Praise for the first edition

"This new book by Duncan Pritchard is an excellent introduction to the theory of knowledge, as well as a useful resource for understanding Pritchard's own important view. Pritchard's treatment of the subject area is masterful, achieving a combination of clarity and efficiency that is rarely seen in philosophy."
– John Greco, *Saint Louis University, USA*

"An excellent overview of contemporary epistemology from the perspective of an established, prolific contributor to the field. It is informative, objective, and well argued, but also readable and engaging."
– Ernest Sosa, *Rutgers University, USA*

Palgrave Philosophy Today

Series Editor: **Vittorio Bufacchi**, University College Cork, Ireland

The *Palgrave Philosophy Today* series provides concise introductions to all the major areas of philosophy currently being taught in philosophy departments around the world. Each book gives a state-of-the-art informed assessment of a key area of philosophical study. In addition, each title in the series offers a distinct interpretation from an outstanding scholar who is closely involved with current work in the field. Books in the series provide students and teachers with not only a succinct introduction to the topic, with the essential information necessary to understand it and the literature being discussed, but also a demanding and engaging entry into the subject.

Titles include:

Helen Beebee
FREE WILL: An Introduction

Shaun Gallagher
PHENOMENOLOGY

Simon Kirchin
METAETHICS

Chad Meister
PHILOSOPHY OF RELIGION

Lilian O'Brien
PHILOSOPHY OF ACTION

Duncan Pritchard
EPISTEMOLOGY

Mathias Risse
GLOBAL POLITICAL PHILOSOPHY

Don Ross
PHILOSOPHY OF ECONOMICS

Joel Walmsley
MIND AND MACHINE

Forthcoming Titles:

Anthony Booth
ANALYTIC ISLAMIC PHILOSOPHY

James Robert Brown
PHILOSOPHY OF SCIENCE

Pascal Engel
PHILOSOPHY OF PSYCHOLOGY

Palgrave Philosophy Today
Series Standing Order ISBN 978–0–230–00232–6 (hardcover)
Series Standing Order ISBN 978–0–230–00233–3 (paperback)
(*outside North America only*)

You can receive future titles in this series as they are published by placing a standing order. Please contact your bookseller or, in case of difficulty, write to us at the address below with your name and address, the title of the series and the ISBN quoted above.

Customer Services Department, Macmillan Distribution Ltd, Houndmills, Basingstoke, Hampshire RG21 6XS, England

Epistemology
2nd edition

Duncan Pritchard
Professor of Philosophy, University of Edinburgh, UK

© Duncan Pritchard 2016

All rights reserved. No reproduction, copy or transmission of this publication may be made without written permission.

No portion of this publication may be reproduced, copied or transmitted save with written permission or in accordance with the provisions of the Copyright, Designs and Patents Act 1988, or under the terms of any licence permitting limited copying issued by the Copyright Licensing Agency, Saffron House, 6–10 Kirby Street, London EC1N 8TS.

Any person who does any unauthorized act in relation to this publication may be liable to criminal prosecution and civil claims for damages.

The author has asserted his right to be identified as the author of this work in accordance with the Copyright, Designs and Patents Act 1988.

First published 2016 by
PALGRAVE MACMILLAN

Palgrave Macmillan in the UK is an imprint of Macmillan Publishers Limited, registered in England, company number 785998, of Houndmills, Basingstoke, Hampshire RG21 6XS.

Palgrave Macmillan in the US is a division of St Martin's Press LLC, 175 Fifth Avenue, New York, NY 10010.

Palgrave Macmillan is the global academic imprint of the above companies and has companies and representatives throughout the world.

Palgrave® and Macmillan® are registered trademarks in the United States, the United Kingdom, Europe and other countries.

ISBN 978-1-137-52690-8 hardback

ISBN 978-1-137-52691-5   ISBN 978-1-137-52692-2 (eBook)
DOI 10.1007/978-1-137-52692-2

This book is printed on paper suitable for recycling and made from fully managed and sustained forest sources. Logging, pulping and manufacturing processes are expected to conform to the environmental regulations of the country of origin.

A catalogue record for this book is available from the British Library.

Library of Congress Cataloging-in-Publication Data

Names: Pritchard, Duncan, author.

Title: Epistemology / Duncan Pritchard.

Other titles: Knowledge

Description: 2nd edition. | New York: Palgrave Macmillan, 2016. | Series: Palgrave philosophy today | Rev. ed. of: Knowledge. c2009. | Includes bibliographical references and index.

Identifiers: LCCN 2015040560| ISBN 978-1-137-52690-8 (hardback) | ISBN 978-1-137-52691-5 (pbk.)

Subjects: LCSH: Knowledge, Theory of.

Classification: LCC BD161 .P7488 2016 | DDC 121—dc23

LC record available at http://lccn.loc.gov/2015040560

For Mandi, Ethan and Alexander

Contents

Series Editor's Preface	ix
Preface	xi

1 Analysing Knowledge — 1
- The project — 1
- The classical account of knowledge — 3
- Gettier-style counterexamples — 6
- No false lemmas — 9
- External and internal epistemic conditions — 10
- The epistemological externalism/internalism distinction — 12
- Chapter summary — 15

2 Anti-Luck Epistemology — 18
- Anti-luck epistemology and the Gettier problem — 18
- Formulating the anti-luck condition I: sensitivity — 19
- Interlude: possible worlds — 20
- Back to sensitivity — 22
- Sensitivity and the lottery problem — 23
- Methods — 24
- Formulating the anti-luck condition II: safety — 26
- Anti-luck epistemology reconsidered — 30
- Robust anti-luck epistemology — 33
- Problems with robust anti-luck epistemology I: necessary propositions — 34
- Problems with robust anti-luck epistemology II: the Temp case — 37
- Concluding remarks — 39
- Chapter summary — 40

3 Virtue Epistemology — 43
- Problems for process reliabilism — 43
- From process reliabilism to virtue epistemology — 44
- Virtue reliabilism versus virtue responsibilism — 46
- Modest virtue epistemology — 48
- Robust virtue epistemology — 50
- Two problems for robust virtue epistemology — 53
- Concluding remarks — 59
- Chapter summary — 59

4 Anti-Luck Virtue Epistemology — 63
Recap — 63
Anti-luck virtue epistemology — 64
The nature of anti-luck virtue epistemology — 68
Diagnosis — 70
Concluding remarks — 74
Chapter summary — 75

5 Epistemic Externalism and Internalism — 77
Introduction — 77
Three internalist theses — 77
Classical *versus* non-classical epistemic internalism — 81
Epistemological disjunctivism — 83
Reflectively accessible factive reasons — 85
Chapter summary — 88

6 Radical Scepticism — 92
Introduction — 92
The closure-based radical sceptical argument — 93
Responding to the closure-based sceptical argument I: denial of the closure principle — 96
Responding to the closure-based sceptical argument II: attributer contextualism — 100
Responding to the closure-based sceptical argument III: neo-Mooreanism — 104
Concluding remarks — 109
Chapter summary — 109

7 Epistemic Value — 112
The value problem for knowledge — 112
The swamping problem — 113
Back to the value problem for knowledge — 116
Knowledge, achievement and final value — 118
Chapter summary — 123

8 Understanding — 126
Introductory remarks — 126
Understanding and knowledge — 127
Understanding and cognitive achievement — 131
Understanding and final value — 133
Concluding remarks — 135
Chapter summary — 135

Bibliography — 139

Index — 145

Series Editor's Preface

It is not easy being a student of philosophy these days. All the different areas of philosophy are reaching ever increasing levels of complexity and sophistication, a fact which is reflected in the specialized literature and readership each branch of philosophy enjoys. And yet, anyone who studies philosophy is expected to have a solid grasp of the most current issues being debated in most, if not all, the other areas of philosophy. It is an understatement to say that students of philosophy today are faced with a Herculean task.

The books in this book series by Palgrave are meant to help all philosophers, established and aspiring, to understand, appreciate and engage with the intricacies which characterize all the many faces of philosophy. They are also ideal teaching tools as textbooks for more advanced students. These books may not be meant primarily for those who have yet to read their first book of philosophy, but all students with a basic knowledge of philosophy will benefit greatly from reading these exciting and original works, which will enable anyone to engage with all the defining issues in contemporary philosophy.

There are three main aspects that make the Palgrave Philosophy Today series distinctive and attractive. First, each book is relatively short. Second, the books are commissioned from some of the best-known, established and upcoming international scholars in each area of philosophy. Third, while the primary purpose is to offer an informed assessment of opinion on a key area of philosophical study, each title presents a distinct interpretation from someone who is closely involved with current work in the field.

This book by Duncan Pritchard on *Epistemology* perfectly reflects the objectives and ambitions of the book series. In the last few years Duncan Pritchard has established himself as one of the most distinctive original voices in epistemology. His books on *Epistemic Luck* (2005), *Epistemological Disjunctivism* (2012) and *Epistemic Angst* (2015) have been the subject of much discussion and unanimous praise, and he is currently playing a central role in defining the agenda in contemporary epistemology for the present generation of philosophers of knowledge.

We are delighted to issue a revised and updated second edition of his 2009 book *Knowledge*, under the new title *Epistemology*, which includes a more in-depth analysis of understanding and the value of knowledge. This edition will make it possible for anyone with an interest in epistemology, novice or expert, to get a sense of where the action is. Covering a vast array of issues, including anti-luck epistemology, virtue epistemology, externalism and internalism about knowledge, radical skepticism and the value of knowledge, Pritchard does more than merely present a running commentary on the major and finer points in the current literature on knowledge; he also makes a distinctive contribution to these debates.

One of the great virtues of this book on knowledge is that Pritchard is much more interested in philosophical *ideas* than in philosophical *figures*. That is the way it should be of course. One of the aims of the Palgrave Studies in Philosophy series is to remind our readers that in philosophy ideas ought to have centre stage.

Vittorio Bufacchi
General Editor, Palgrave Philosophy Today
Department of Philosophy
University College Cork, Ireland
v.bufacchi@ucc.ie

Preface

This book is the (re-titled) second edition of *Knowledge* (Palgrave Macmillan 2009). The reason for the re-titling is that it more accurately represents the content covered, particularly now that I've extended the book by writing new distinct chapters on epistemic value and understanding. Otherwise, the main changes in the transition from first to second addition have been concerned with 'refreshing' the text (textbooks get stale very quickly) and adding a bunch of useful pedagogical features (every chapter now has a chapter summary, annotated lists of introductory readings, advanced readings, free internet resources, and additional lists of study questions and sample essay questions). What I've tried to preserve from the first edition is the idea of this being a text on contemporary epistemology which presents a coherent narrative arc through some of the key issues in this area. As such, I haven't aimed at offering a broad comprehensive sweep of *all* the issues (which means that I've left out some significant contemporary debates), and I've completely ignored the history of the subject (important though it is). There is a place for gargantuan texts which have these grander designs, but there is also a place for more concise works that cover a fundamental cross-section of pivotal contemporary issues in an area and nothing more. This book – both first and second edition – falls clearly into the latter category.

One unusual aspect of the first edition that I have preserved in the second edition is that I have continued to resist the scholarly urge to discuss philosophical *figures* in the main text (except where it is unavoidable) and have opted instead to focus solely on the *ideas*. The rationale for this is that it is the ideas after all that are our primary concern. Moreover, by doing things this way one can offer a cleaner and more straightforward summary of the literature, since one does not need to get bogged down by exploring those nuances which separate one philosopher's view from another's that don't have any significance for the wider philosophical debate. In any case, at the end of each chapter there is a detailed summary of where to look to find out who said what, so the reader will not be missing out on anything.

One final feature of the book (both first and second edition) that I want to flag is that although I've tried to present the ground covered here in a generally impartial way, I've also not hesitated in making my own views clear at key junctures. My hope is that this will make the book of more interest to the reader; it's certainly true that as a student I found books written in this way more philosophically stimulating than their more coy counterparts. In any case, the people who pick up this book will surely know – or at least ought to know – that they should not defer to authority (to the extent that anyone in philosophy, much less I, counts as an authority).

A further advantage of writing in this way is that it affords one scope to do more than merely *report* what is happening in the field. Indeed, my goal in the first edition was to write an accessible text on contemporary epistemology which actually *contributed* to the area; which *advanced* the debate. Since that edition came out, I've been pleased to see how often it gets referenced in scholarly articles. Only time will tell if the second edition will be as successful in this regard, but I can at least say this much: as with the first edition, it was surprisingly good fun trying.

1
Analysing Knowledge

The project

The principal concern of epistemology has tended to be the philosophical exploration of propositional knowledge (i.e., *knowledge that* such-and-such is the case), where this involves offering an analysis of this notion. Call this the *analytic project*. In this book, we will be following mainstream epistemology in focussing on the analytical project. (Note that, henceforth, when I talk about 'knowledge' without qualification it will be propositional knowledge that I have in mind.) Even if one grants that it is right to make propositional knowledge our focus (some have questioned this), there are two (as we will see, inter-related) worries about the analytic project that we should consider from the outset (we will consider a third worry presently). The first is whether knowledge is the kind of thing that one can analyse in the first place. The second is what it means to offer an analysis of knowledge. Let us start with the second worry, since I think this will shed some light on why we need not be overly concerned about the first worry.

One very austere way of understanding the analytic project is that what we are seeking are necessary and sufficient conditions that capture our everyday, or 'folk', usage of the term – i.e., which don't conflict with any of our folk talk regarding when someone counts as having knowledge. I think it ought to be clear that such a project is pretty hopeless. For one thing, there is very little reason to think that our folk usage is going to be disciplined enough such that it generates an extension that a particular set of necessary and sufficient conditions could capture. In any case, I think it is natural, from a theoretical perspective, to not take some of our folk employments of terms at face-value. For example, one quite often hears people saying that they knew a falsehood – e.g., the loser in a competition says that he just *knew* he was going to win – and yet we have a very strong intuition about knowledge that one cannot know falsehoods. In such cases, the natural thing to do is to try to explain away the awkward linguistic data – e.g., by arguing that such assertions should not be interpreted literally.

Clearly, however, we do not want to offer an analysis of a term that is completely theoretical – i.e., which is completely divorced from everyday folk usage. If we took that route, then it is hard to see why we should describe the analysandum as being knowledge at all. What we are after, then, is an analysis which is anchored in our everyday usage but which is suitably 'cleaned-up', and is in this sense the product of theory. Of course, this doesn't mean that we can summarily dismiss any recalcitrant linguistic data uttered by the folk, since it is incumbent upon us to explain away this data in a compelling manner where applicable. The point is just that we should not think that our project is hostage to this data in the way that the overly austere conception of the analytic project suggests.

This, at any rate, is how I am understanding the analytic project here. Note that this way of understanding the matter could equally be described as an analysis that captures what is central to our folk usage – i.e., the paradigmatic use of this term. Either way, what is important is that this is a relatively modest theoretical ambition when compared with the austere reading of the analytic project. Moreover, with this modesty of ambition in mind, it becomes far more plausible that knowledge may well succumb to an analysis. That is, if one held to the more austere rendering of this project, then one would tend to be very depressed about its prospects since apparent counterexamples to any putative set of necessary and sufficient conditions would be very easy to find. But once one moves away from the austere reading of the analytic project, then such counterexamples cease to be so readily available.

Note, by the way, that I am here taking it for granted that, ideally, any analysis of knowledge will be *reductive*, in the sense that it would analyse knowledge in terms that don't make essential use of the concept of knowledge itself. It might well turn out that this isn't possible. If that happens, then that doesn't mean that we should thereby abandon the analytic project altogether, since even circular analyses can be informative – just as non-circular analyses can sometimes be trivial – and it could also be helpful to know what the core necessary conditions of knowledge are. (We will consider an example of an informative but circular analysis of knowledge in chapter four).

Still, a failure to offer a reductive analysis of knowledge might make us wonder whether we should reverse the direction of explanation. As some have argued, perhaps we should treat knowledge as a *primitive* notion that we should use to define other key epistemic terms. This is what is sometimes called 'knowledge-first' epistemology. Rather than directly arguing against this view, I think it is better to simply proceed with the analytic project, modestly conceived, and try to show that such a project can generate some plausible proposals. This is what I will do in this book.

Nevertheless, as we proceed we will see that I have some sympathy with a third concern about the analytic project. This worry is that by making this project central to epistemology one thereby unduly skews one's understanding of the subject matter such that one is prevented from taking seriously other epistemic standings that don't play a role in one's theory of knowledge. This worry arises because what tends to be presupposed by the analytic project is that knowledge is the central epistemological term, and thus that the more general project of epistemological analysis should be centred on the analytic project. I think it is right to be suspicious of this presupposition, and I will explain why at a later point. As we will see however, that this presupposition is suspect does not mitigate against pursuing the analytic project since we can only properly draw out why this presupposition is dubious by getting a clearer grip on the nature of knowledge.

With the foregoing in mind, we will begin.

The classical account of knowledge

The contemporary debate regarding how to analyse knowledge largely takes its cue from a famous three-page article published by Edmund Gettier (1963). In this paper, Gettier argues that the classical three-part (or 'tripartite') account of knowledge is fatally flawed. This conception of knowledge holds that there are three conditions to knowledge, all of which are individually necessary and jointly sufficient for knowledge:

The Classical Account of Knowledge
An agent S knows that p if, and only if, (i) S believes that p, (ii) S's belief that p is true, and (iii) S's belief that p is justified.

Let's start with the first two conditions, since these are the least contentious. First, there is the *doxastic* condition that knowledge demands belief. If you know that the moon is not made of cheese, then you must at least believe this. Suppose, for example, that you went around saying that the moon was made of Stilton (which you are clearly aware is a type of cheese) and, when it was pointed out to you that the moon was not made of cheese, you claimed that you knew that all along. In such a case we would argue that you couldn't have known what you claimed to have known because you didn't even believe it. (Note that sometimes we talk as if one can have knowledge without belief, as when we say things like 'I don't believe it, I *know* it', but expressions like this seem to be just shorthand for saying 'I don't *just* believe it, I *know* it').

Next, consider the *factivity* condition that knowledge demands truth. We might *think* we know all sorts of propositions that are false, but if they really are false then we don't know these propositions after all. Thinking that you know something is not the same as knowing it. We only credit knowledge to someone when what that person believes is true. (Again, and as noted above, we do sometimes say that we knew falsehoods, as when one says that one just knew that one was going to win a competition which one in fact lost. On closer inspection, however, assertions like this seem shorthand for saying that one was very confident, perhaps even rightly so, that one knew the target proposition, a claim which is compatible with the factivity of knowledge).

Clearly, however, there is more to knowledge than mere true belief. After all, one can form a true belief in an entirely inappropriate fashion, from an epistemic point of view, and hence it would not count as knowledge. Consider, for example, the following case:

Gullible John
Gullible John forms his beliefs by always uncritically trusting the word of others. Knowing how gullible he is, his friends decide to play a prank on him and tell him that the moon is made of cheese. Since he believes whatever he is told he comes in this way to believe that this is the case. As it happens, however, and unbeknownst to anyone, it turns out that the moon is indeed made of cheese.

Does Gullible John's true belief qualify as knowledge? Surely not. After all, it is simply a matter of luck that his belief is true; it certainly doesn't reflect any cognitive ability on John's part.

In contrast, consider a parallel case where the agent does have knowledge:

Scientist Joan
Scientist Joan is a top scientist who has been chosen to make a space mission to the moon to determine what it is made of. While there she carefully and successfully undertakes a number of experiments and discovers, to her surprise, that the moon is made of cheese. Consequently, she forms the true belief that the moon is made of cheese.

Intuitively, Scientist Joan *does* have knowledge of what she believes. This prompts the question of what it is about Scientist Joan that sets her apart from Gullible John such that she has knowledge that Gullible John lacks?

According to the classical account of knowledge, the answer to this question is that it is only Scientist Joan who is *justified* in what she believes, where this means that she is able to offer sufficient good reasons in favour of her belief (i.e., good reasons for thinking that this belief is true). In contrast, Gullible John is unable to offer any good reasons in favour of his belief, and hence we can account for why he lacks knowledge by pointing to the fact that he lacks a justification for his belief. Pairs of cases like this thus seem to support the classical account of knowledge. More generally, it does seem right to say that knowledge demands justification in just this sense. For example, when someone claims to know something we expect them to be able to back up what they say with good reasons. If, in contrast, they were unable to do this – were unable to offer any reasons in support of what they believe, say, or offered manifestly poor ones – then we would regard them as lacking knowledge, and treat their original claim to know as false.

The classical account of knowledge thus appears to offer a very straightforward way of thinking about knowledge, one that has a lot of intuitive appeal. Note also that what makes it so appealing is that it seems able to comfortably accommodate two overarching epistemological intuitions that we just appealed to when we were discussing knowledge. The first is that knowledge in some sense excludes luck. That is, one cannot, like Gullible John, gain knowledge simply by having a true belief that is only true as a matter of luck. Put another way, this is the intuition that when one has knowledge one's true belief in the target proposition could not have easily been wrong. Call this the *anti-luck intuition* about knowledge. The second is that knowledge is in some sense the product of cognitive ability. That is, the reason why Scientist Joan, who discovers that the moon is made of cheese through proper scientific investigation, has knowledge (but Gullible John doesn't) is that she acquired her true belief through the exercise of her cognitive abilities (e.g., her scientific expertise). Call this the *ability intuition* about knowledge.

As we will see as we go along, these two intuitions have had a tremendous effect on contemporary theorising about knowledge. How they are best understood, and how they are related to one another, are questions that we will return to later on. For now though, I simply want to register their intuitive force and also the fact that the classical account of knowledge seems excellently placed to accommodate both of them. After all, if one's true belief is supported by excellent reasons, then why would it be merely a matter of luck that one's belief is true? Moreover, if one can offer excellent reasons in support of what one believes, then doesn't it immediately follow that one's true belief is the product of one's cognitive ability?

Gettier-style counterexamples

Unfortunately, despite the surface appeal of the classical account of knowledge, Gettier demonstrated that it was unsustainable in its current form. Here is one of the counterexamples that Gettier offered.

> *Smith and Jones*
> Smith and Jones have both applied for a job. Smith has good reason to believe both that Jones will get the job (the head of the appointing committee told him this, say), and that Jones has ten coins in his pocket (perhaps he saw him put the coins in his pocket himself). He is thus justified in believing this conjunction. Accordingly, Smith infers that the person who will get the job has ten coins in his pocket. It is not Jones who gets the job, however, but Smith. Nevertheless, Smith's belief that the person who will get the job has ten coins in his pocket is still true since, unbeknownst to Smith, he has ten coins in his pocket.

Given how Smith came to form this belief, it is surely justified since he can offer excellent reasons in its favour. Given that his belief is also true, he thus has a justified true belief and hence, according to the classical account of knowledge, he has knowledge. Crucially, however, we would not say that Smith's justified true belief amounts to knowledge, and the reason for this is that it is just too lucky that his belief is true. In particular, that Smith's belief is true has nothing to do with the reasons that he is able to offer in its favour.

The general form of a Gettier-style counterexample is that it takes a belief that is formed in such a way that, while justified, it would ordinarily have been false, and then adds a further flourish to the example to ensure that the belief is true nonetheless, albeit not in a way that is connected to the justification the agent has for her belief. The upshot of such cases is that the agent, while having a justified true belief, nonetheless has a belief that is only true as a matter of luck. In particular, given how Smith's belief was formed, it could have easily been false (e.g., if he had only nine coins in his pocket). Gettier-style cases thus primarily offend against the anti-luck intuition about knowledge.

So, in the case just given, for example, Smith forms his belief that the person who will get the job has ten coins in his pocket by inferring it from a false conjunction (that Jones will get the job and that Jones has ten coins in his pocket, the first conjunct of which is false). Ordinarily, drawing an inference from a false belief would result in a further false belief. Nonetheless, the belief in this case is justified for, as this case illustrates, one can have good reason to believe something even where one formed one's belief in a way that would ordinarily result in a falsehood. Finally, the twist in the story is that Smith's belief is true nonetheless, albeit true in a way that is completely unconnected with the justification that Smith has for his belief. As a result, Smith's belief, while justified and true, is only true as a matter of luck.

The case just given essentially appeals to an inference from a false belief. Interestingly, however, it seems that this feature of the case is not essential. Consider the following example:

Roddy
Roddy is a farmer. One day he is looking into a field near-by and clearly sees something that looks just like a sheep. Consequently, he forms a belief that there is a sheep in the field. Moreover, this belief is true, in that there is a sheep in the field in question. But what Roddy is looking at is not a sheep, however, but a big hairy dog that looks just like a sheep and which is obscuring from view the sheep standing just behind.

Given that Roddy is a farmer, and given also that he gets to have such a good look at the sheep-shaped object in question, it ought to be uncontentious to suppose that he has excellent grounds for believing what he does, and hence that his belief is justified. Since his belief is also true, he therefore has a justified true belief and hence, according to the classical account of knowledge at any rate, he ought to have knowledge of what he believes. Clearly, though, this is not the case since Roddy cannot gain knowledge that there is a sheep in a field by looking at a big hairy dog, even if his justified belief happens, by luck, to be true.

Again, then, we have a counterexample to the classical account of knowledge, in that we have a justified true belief that does not appear to be a case of knowledge. This example also has the general structure of a Gettier-style case. Roddy forms his belief in a manner such that, while justified, it would ordinarily have been false – one would not normally form a true belief that there is a sheep in a field by looking at a big hairy dog. By chance, however, his belief is true regardless, though in a way that is completely unconnected to the justification he has for his belief. What is significant about the example for our purposes is that there is no obvious inference taking place here as we find in the Smith and Jones example that Gettier offers. After all, Roddy simply forms the belief that there is a sheep in the field by looking at the sheep-shaped object (i.e., the big hairy dog).

There is also a third kind of Gettier-style case that we should note. This case is like the Roddy case just given in that it involves perceptual belief. Unlike the Roddy case, however, the agent really does see the target object.

Barney
Barney is driving through the country and happens to look out of the window into a field that he is driving past. In doing so, he gets to have a good look at a barn-shaped object, whereupon he forms the belief that there is barn in the field. This belief is true, since what he is looking at really is a barn. Unbeknownst to Barney, however, he is presently in 'barn façade county' where every other object that looks like a barn is actually a clever fake. Had Barney looked at one of the fake barns, then he would not have noticed the difference. Quite by chance, however, Barney just happened to look at the one real barn in the vicinity.

Given that Barney gets such a good look at the barn and has no reason to suspect that he is in barn façade county, we ought to be able to grant that he has excellent grounds in support of what he believes, and so is justified in what he believes. Moreover, the belief that he forms is true, in that there really is a barn in front of him. Barney thus has a justified true belief and hence, according to the classical account of knowledge, he has knowledge too. Clearly, though, Barney cannot come to know that he is looking at a barn in this case.

The reason for this, in common with all Gettier-style cases, is that it is just too lucky that his belief is true – he could so very easily have been mistaken in this case (i.e., if he's looked at one of the fake barns instead). As with other Gettier-style cases, Barney is forming his belief in a way such that, while justified, his belief would ordinarily be false – taking a barn-shaped object to be a barn is a very unreliable of forming a belief about whether what one is looking at is a barn when one is in barn façade county. Nonetheless, his belief is true, albeit in such a way that it is unconnected to the justification he has for his belief (i.e., his grounds for thinking that this is a barn – basically, that it looks like a barn – in no way distinguish between barns and barn-façades).

Like the Roddy case, this example doesn't obviously seem to involve any inference on the part of the agent. There is also a further difference, however, which is that Barney really does get to see the object in question. That is, while Roddy isn't actually looking at a sheep (but rather a big hairy dog that looks just like a sheep), Barney really is looking at a barn. This means that it isn't even essential to Gettier-style cases that one is in any way in error in how one forms one's belief; all that is essential is that the justified true belief in question is only true as a matter of luck.

No false lemmas

Gettier-style cases thus demonstrate that the classical account of knowledge is wrong. This therefore poses a problem for contemporary epistemology, which is that if this very intuitive account of knowledge is wrong, then what is the right account of knowledge to go for? In particular, how should one go about formulating a theory of knowledge which is Gettier-proof? This is the *Gettier problem*.

Early responses to the Gettier problem assumed that all that was needed was an extra flourish to the tripartite account in order to rescue it. For example, some focussed on the fact that Gettier's own examples seem to involve agents making inferences from a false premise or assumption. Accordingly, one might naturally argue that the solution to the problem is just to argue that knowledge is justified true belief that is not based on any false premises or assumptions (or 'lemmas'). This is the *no false lemmas* response to the Gettier problem. Thus, Smith lacks knowledge that the person who will get the job has ten coins in his pocket because his belief, while justified and true, is based on a false assumption (that Jones will get the job).

There are two inter-related problems with this sort of response. The first is that one can construct Gettier-style examples where there seems to be no inference involved at all. Neither the Roddy case nor the Barney case described above obviously involves the agent making any kind of inference. It is thus incumbent on the proponent of this view to offer a notion of an 'assumption' that is applicable even to these cases.

The second problem is that we tend to assume an awful lot when we form our beliefs, and it therefore seems highly likely that some of what we assume will be false. Accordingly, this account of knowledge seems to set the standards for knowledge far too high. Suppose, for example, that when Scientist Joan was conducting one of her hundred-or-so experiments on the moon rock in order to determine whether the moon was made of cheese a machine that she thought was working okay was in fact malfunctioning and so didn't give her the right reading. As it happens this reading, while wrong, was consistent with the hypothesis that the substance that she was investigating was cheese. So Scientist Joan forms her belief that the moon is made of cheese partly on the assumption that this machine gave her the right reading, but this assumption is false. Does this mean that she doesn't know that the moon is made of cheese? Intuitively not, since she made many investigations, and this failed experiment was only a small aspect of her studies on the moon rock. Knowledge is thus consistent with *some* false assumptions, provided that they are relatively minor.

These two problems are interconnected, since whatever one might say in response to the one problem will make it more difficult to respond to the other problem. The first problem, after all, prompts the proponent of the no false lemmas view to loosen the notion of assumption in play, so that it can be applicable even to cases like the Roddy or Barney case. But the second problem, in contrast, calls on the proponent of the no false lemmas account to offer a more restricted account of what they mean by an assumption, so that the peripheral false assumption made by Scientist Joan doesn't undermine her knowledge. The challenge for the defender of the no false lemmas proposal is thus to offer a principled way of thinking about assumptions such that it is both not so restrictive that it can't deal with all Gettier-style cases, and which is at the same time not so permissive that it undermines *bona fide* knowledge. That's a very tall order, and thus far no one has successfully managed this.

External and internal epistemic conditions

The no false lemmas response to the Gettier problem essentially proceeds by supposing that the classical account of knowledge is basically right, it's just that it needs to be refined in some way to deal with Gettier-style cases. Any response to the Gettier problem which holds that knowledge is justified true belief plus an anti-Gettier condition (or conditions) will be of this conservative sort (we will consider some other proposals in this vein later on). In light of the Gettier problem, however, one might start to wonder whether what is required is something more than such a mere 'tweaking' of the classical account.

In order to see what is at issue here, we need to introduce a distinction between internal and external epistemic conditions. An *epistemic condition* is a condition that one adds to true belief, perhaps in conjunction with other epistemic conditions, in order to get knowledge. On the classical account of knowledge, then, there is just one epistemic condition, and it is the justification condition. What makes an epistemic condition internal is that the facts that determine that the agent has satisfied that condition are accessible to the agent by reflection alone (i.e., the agent can come to know them by introspection and *a priori* reasoning alone, and needn't undertake any further empirical inquiry). On this conception of an internal epistemic condition, justification on the classical account of knowledge is an internal epistemic condition. After all, what makes you justified is that you are in possession of good reasons in support of your belief. Crucially, though, on the classical account to be in possession of such good reasons means being able to cite them. Thus, one ought to have no problem accessing those reasons by reflection alone.

An external epistemic condition, in contrast, is any epistemic condition that is not an internal epistemic condition – i.e., the facts that determine that the agent has satisfied that condition are *not* always accessible to the agent by reflection alone. The no false lemmas response to the Gettier problem, like all conservative responses to the Gettier problem, is in effect claiming that in order to have knowledge one needs to have a true belief that satisfies both an internal epistemic condition (justification) and an external epistemic condition (no false lemmas). After all, whether the relevant assumptions that are in play when forming one's belief are true will not normally be something that one can know by reflection alone, since it depends on how the world in fact is (i.e., and not on how one thinks the world is, whether reasonably or otherwise).

It is important to note why the Gettier-style cases require us to at the very least add an external epistemic condition to our theory of knowledge. In short, and this is something that Gettier himself notes in his famous article, the reason why the classical justification condition seems to generate Getter-style cases is because no matter how good one's justification is for believing a proposition, that proposition could nevertheless be false. As a result, it is inevitable that the classical account of knowledge will be subject to Gettier-style cases because – as we noted above – all one needs to do is consider a case in which the agent's justified belief is formed in such a way that it would ordinarily be false and then simply make the belief true regardless, albeit in a way that is unconnected to the agent's justification. Intuitively, what goes for the justification condition, classically conceived, will go for any internal epistemic condition, since what one has reflective access to will only be one's own mental states – e.g., what one believes about the world – and yet there is no guarantee that our mental states will match up with the facts in the world. We will come back to consider this point in more detail in chapter five, where we will offer a more nuanced account of the epistemic internalism/externalism distinction.

For now, it suffices to note that the immediate moral of the Gettier problem seems to be that the prospects for any theory of knowledge that only has internal epistemic conditions are dim indeed. With this point in mind, one might start to wonder if one should incorporate internal epistemic conditions into one's theory of knowledge at all.

The epistemological externalism/internalism distinction

Here is where we encounter a distinction that is central to contemporary epistemology between internalist and externalist theories of knowledge. The standard way of drawing this distinction is that an internalist theory of knowledge is any theory of knowledge that incorporates at least one internal epistemic condition (usually the classical justification condition). In contrast, an externalist theory of knowledge is any theory of knowledge that isn't an internalist theory of knowledge – i.e., which doesn't insist on there being an internal epistemic condition.

On this way of drawing the distinction, the classical account of knowledge is a very strong internalist theory of knowledge, since it only has one epistemic condition and that is an internal epistemic condition. The Gettier problem seems to show that any strong internalist theory of knowledge of this sort is untenable. What the Gettier problem doesn't show, however, is that internalism in the theory of knowledge is untenable. Suppose one had a view that held that knowledge is justified true belief which meets some further external epistemic condition, and suppose further that this further external epistemic condition could deal with all the Gettier-style cases. Such a view would then be immune to the Gettier problem. Crucially, however, it would still be an internalist theory of knowledge because it insists on the satisfaction of an internalist epistemic condition (justification).

Nevertheless, one might be tempted to respond to the Gettier problem in a more radical fashion by looking for an external epistemic condition or conditions that sufficed, with true belief, for knowledge. If one held such a position then one would opting for epistemic externalism about knowledge.

An example of such a proposal, a view that we will examine more closely in the next chapter, is *process reliabilism*. According to process reliabilism – in its simplest form at any rate – knowledge is true belief that is the product of a reliable process, where a reliable process is a process that tends to result in true beliefs. The epistemic condition laid down by the reliabilist is clearly an external epistemic condition since one cannot know by reflection alone that one's belief is formed in a reliable fashion (one can know by reflection alone that one has good reason to think that one's belief is formed in a reliable fashion, but that's a different matter entirely).

Now process reliabilism, at least in the simple form just considered (we will consider some more complex versions in the next chapter), is unable to deal with all Gettier-style cases. After all, the agents in the Gettier-style examples described above are all arguably forming their respective beliefs in the target proposition in a reliable fashion. In the Smith and Jones case, for example, inferring one's belief from a prior belief that one has excellent reason to believe is true is surely a reliable way of forming a belief. Similarly, in each of the Roddy and Barney cases the agent seems to be forming his belief in the target proposition in a reliable fashion. So process reliabilism by itself won't solve the Gettier problem. Still, as we will see in the next chapter, there are more subtle versions of this thesis that may be able to deal with this problem. What is interesting for our purposes, however, is not the fact that this view (suitably modified perhaps) may or may not be able to deal with the Gettier problem, but the fact that, as an externalist account of knowledge, it represents a radical departure from the kind of epistemic internalism that is central to the classical account of knowledge, and which lives on in post-Gettier internalist theories of knowledge (such as the view that knowledge is justified true belief plus a no false lemmas condition).

So why might one be attracted to an externalist theory of knowledge? Well, for one thing there do seem to be certain cases of knowledge that aren't well captured by internalist theories of knowledge. Consider the following case:

Chuck
Chuck has a highly reliable ability to distinguish between male and female chicks, a skill that he has acquired by being raised around chicks. He's doesn't know how he does this – he thinks it might be through sight and touch, but he's not sure – and he also hasn't taken the trouble to verify that his ability really is reliable (he just takes it for granted that it is). Still, if you want to know whether a chick is male or female, you go see Chuck and he'll tell you.

Does Chuck have knowledge? Here is where externalists and internalists about knowledge diverge. In favour of epistemic externalism, notice that the true beliefs formed by Chuck respect both of the two core intuitions that we noted about knowledge above. On the one hand, the beliefs are clearly a product of genuine cognitive ability, since it is stipulated that he does indeed have the ability to reliably tell male and female chicks apart. Thus, the true beliefs in question don't contravene the ability intuition about knowledge. Moreover, the true beliefs formed by Chuck clearly aren't true as a matter of luck, given that they are indeed formed as a result of a genuine cognitive ability. Thus, the true beliefs in question don't contravene the anti-luck intuition about knowledge either. There are, then, some compelling grounds for supposing that the true beliefs formed by Chuck should qualify as knowledge.

In opposition to this, internalists about knowledge insist that merely forming one's belief in a way that is in fact reliable shouldn't suffice for knowledge, for what is required in addition is some reflective grasp of one's epistemic situation. That is, the internalist about knowledge argues that externalism unduly allows knowledge to be completely opaque to the agent by enabling agents to have knowledge even in the absence of supporting reflectively accessible grounds.

The Chuck case is clearly a divisive example, in that those who aren't already sympathetic to externalism about knowledge are unlikely to be persuaded by it. Are there any other reasons why one might be attracted to externalism about knowledge? Well, one reason might be that internalist theories of knowledge could be accused of over-intellectualising knowledge. After all, we often ascribe knowledge to 'agents' (the reason for the scare quotes will become apparent in a moment) who are not in a position to cite good reasons in favour of their beliefs. Think, for example, of small children or, indeed, higher-order mammals (and perhaps some not so higher-order mammals too). Of course, the proponent of the internalist theory of knowledge could argue that such ascriptions should not be taken at face-value. Perhaps, for example, the 'knowledge' that we credit to, say, small children is not *bona fide* knowledge at all but rather a kind of proto-knowledge.

There is a lot more to be said about the epistemic externalism/internalism distinction as it applies to knowledge. For now, however, what is important is only that we register this distinction and its importance. As we go along, we will explore this distinction, and its implications for contemporary epistemology, in more detail.

Chapter summary

In this chapter we have encountered the *analytical project* in epistemology, which is the challenge of offering an analysis of propositional knowledge. We noted that there are two relatively uncontroversial conditions on knowledge – viz., that it entails both truth (the *factivity* condition) and belief (the *doxastic* condition). But we also saw that mere true belief does not suffice for knowledge, as one can form true beliefs in ways that are manifestly inappropriate from an epistemic point of view (e.g., via mere gullibility). In particular, knowledge excludes lucky success, in the sense that one has a true belief that could very easily have been wrong (the *anti-luck intuition*). It also demands that one's true belief should be in some way the product of one's cognitive ability (the *ability intuition*). The *classical account of knowledge*, which is the view that knowledge is justified true belief, initially seemed to offer a complete account of knowledge, but ultimately succumbed to the *Gettier-style cases*. These are cases in which a subject has a justified true belief, but where her true belief is even so merely a matter of luck. Hence, the subject lacks knowledge. We saw that there are several kinds of Gettier-style case, some involving inference, some involving non-inferential perceptual belief, and even some involving non-inferential veridical perceptual belief (i.e., where one is not mistaken about what one sees, as in the Barney case). The challenge of constructing a theory of knowledge that excludes these Gettier-style cases is the *Gettier problem*. We examined one flawed way of responding to the Gettier problem, which was the *no false lemmas* proposal according to which knowledge is justified true belief that is based on no false assumptions. We explored the distinction between *internal and external epistemic conditions*, where the justification condition in the classical account of knowledge is a good example of the former and the no false lemmas condition is a good example of the latter. Finally, we encountered the distinction between *internalist and externalist theories of knowledge*, where the former is any theory of knowledge that includes an internal epistemic condition, and the latter is any theory of knowledge that does not include an internal epistemic condition. We considered some of the motivations that one might offer for epistemic externalism about knowledge.

Further introductory reading

For an introductory overview of the main topics covered in this chapter, see Pritchard (2013, Chapters 1–6). See also Pritchard (2009a), Hetherington (2011), and Pritchard (2015c, §4). See Turri (2011) for an excellent annotated bibliography of materials on the nature of knowledge. See also the readings listed below under 'free internet resources', particularly Hetherington (2015).

Further advanced reading

For an interesting recent discussion of what the target of a philosophical analysis should be, see the exchange between Goldman (2007) and Kornblith (2007). See also Weatherson (2003) and Pritchard (2012c). For the main defence of knowledge-first epistemology, which includes grounds for scepticism about the very project of analysing knowledge, see Williamson (2000). For a recent critique of knowledge-first epistemology, see McGlynn (2014). See also Craig (1991). For further discussion of Gettier-style counterexamples to the classical account of knowledge, see Zagzebski (1999). The Roddy case is described in Chisholm (1989). The Barney case is described in Goldman (1976), and credited to Carl Ginet. For a response to the Gettier problem that is roughly along the lines of the no false lemmas response, see Lehrer (1965). For further discussion of the epistemic externalism/internalism distinction, see the papers collected in Kornblith (2001). The main proponent of (a version of) process reliabilism is Goldman (e.g., 1986).

Free internet resources

For more on the general issue of the analysis of knowledge, see Ichikawa & Steup (2012) and Hetherington (2015). See also Steup (2005) and Truncellito (2007). For further discussion of Gettier-style counterexamples to the classical account of knowledge, see Hetherington (2005). Gettier's (1963) article is widely available on the internet.

Study questions

1 What is *propositional* knowledge, and how might it differ from other kinds of knowledge (e.g., *ability knowledge*, otherwise known as know-how, or *acquaintance knowledge*)?

2 Why is mere true belief not sufficient for knowledge?
3 What are the anti-luck and ability intuitions about knowledge? How plausible do you find them?
4 What is the classical account of knowledge? How does the classical account of knowledge explain why a lucky true belief doesn't count as knowledge?
5 What is a Gettier-style example, and what do such cases show? Try to formulate a Gettier-style case of your own.
6 In what way might it be said that the problem with Gettier-style cases is that they involve a justified true belief that is based on a false assumption?
7 What is the no false lemmas response to the Gettier problem? What, if anything, is wrong with it?
8 What is an epistemic condition, and what makes an epistemic condition either internalist or externalist?
9 What makes a theory of knowledge externalist? What kinds of considerations motivate epistemic externalism about knowledge? Do you find any of them compelling?

Sample essay questions
1 Explain, in detail, the problem posed for the classical account of knowledge by Gettier-style cases. Should this account of knowledge be abandoned altogether as a result, or can it survive in an amended form?
2 Describe, and critically evaluate, the no false lemmas response to the Gettier problem.
3 'Justification is neither necessary nor sufficient for knowledge.' Discuss.

2
Anti-Luck Epistemology

Anti-luck epistemology and the Gettier problem

In the last chapter we encountered the Gettier problem that is posed by the Gettier-style cases. This is the problem of how to formulate a theory of knowledge which is 'Gettier-proof'. We noted that Gettier-style cases essentially trade on the anti-luck intuition that if one has knowledge then one has a true belief that could not have easily been wrong. In light of this fact, one natural thought to have is that rather than fixating on avoiding Gettier-style cases we should instead try to formulate that epistemic condition (or conditions) which appropriately accommodates the anti-luck intuition – i.e., we should try to formulate the *anti-luck epistemic condition*. After all, if we were able to formulate such a condition, then that would deal with the Gettier problem by default, plus any other cases that trade on the anti-luck intuition. We will call any theory of knowledge that explicitly has as a central component an anti-luck epistemic condition an *anti-luck epistemology*. That the condition has to be explicitly thought of in this way is important since all theories of knowledge aim to exclude knowledge-undermining epistemic luck, and so all such theories can be thought of as implicitly incorporating an anti-luck epistemic condition. Nevertheless, only some theories *explicitly* incorporate such a condition, as we will see.

We can also distinguish between *modest* and *robust* versions of anti-luck epistemology. A robust anti-luck epistemology will hold that once we have formulated the anti-luck condition, then there is no more work for the epistemologist to do. On this view, then, knowledge just is true belief plus the anti-luck epistemic condition. Since we have other intuitions about knowledge other than the anti-luck intuition – in particular, as we saw in the last chapter, we have the intuition that knowledge involves true belief that is the product of the agent's cognitive ability (the *ability intuition*) – it follows that on this view the idea is that these other intuitions about knowledge are in effect reducible to the anti-luck intuition. For example, one might hold that the reason why we care that knowledge involves a true belief that is the product of the agent's cognitive ability is because we care about excluding knowledge-undermining epistemic luck from our beliefs – and beliefs formed by one's cognitive abilities tend not to be luckily true.

In contrast, modest anti-luck epistemology holds that the anti-luck epistemic condition, while a central epistemic condition, does not suffice by itself to turn true belief into knowledge. Instead, a further condition is required. As we will see, the anti-luck epistemic condition, however it is formulated, is an external epistemic condition in the sense defined in the last chapter (that is, such that one is unable to tell by reflection alone that one has satisfied such a condition). Accordingly, robust anti-luck epistemology is committed to externalism in the theory of knowledge. Whether or not modest anti-luck epistemology is also committed to externalism about knowledge depends on whether the additional epistemic condition that it imposes on knowledge (or at least one of those additional epistemic conditions, if there is more than one) is an internal epistemic condition, like the justification condition that formed part of the classical account of knowledge.

Formulating the anti-luck condition I: sensitivity

So how should one formulate the anti-luck condition? There have been two main proposals in the literature. The first appeals to a principle called the *sensitivity principle*. Here is a rough statement of this principle:

The Sensitivity Principle
If S knows that p, then S's true belief that p is such that, had p been false, then S would not have believed that p.

The basic idea behind the sensitivity principle is that when it comes to knowledge we don't simply want a belief that matches up with the facts – i.e., which is true – but also a belief that is *sensitive* to the facts, such that one wouldn't have believed what one did had it been false.

Before we get into the detail of what this principle demands, it is useful to first evaluate it on an intuitive level. Consider the Roddy case that we looked at in the last chapter. Here we have an agent who has a true belief but who does not qualify for knowledge because his belief is true as a matter of luck (his belief is only true because there just happens to be a sheep hidden from view behind the sheep-shaped object – the big hairy dog – that he's looking at). Notice, though, that we can explain why Roddy doesn't have knowledge in terms of the sensitivity principle since his belief is clearly insensitive. That is, had what he believed been false – i.e., if there hadn't been a sheep hidden from view behind the sheep-shaped object that he's looking at – then he would have continued to have believed that there was a sheep in the field regardless, and so formed a false belief. Moreover, notice that if Roddy had formed his belief by actually looking at a sheep in the normal way, then his belief would have been sensitive: had what he believed not been true – i.e., if there wasn't a sheep before him – then he wouldn't have believed that there is a sheep in the field, and so he wouldn't have ended up forming a false belief.

Sensitivity is able to deal with lots of other cases in this way. One might naturally ask, however, how one is supposed to read this principle. After all, it's all very well appealing to an intuitive notion of how a belief might be sensitive to the facts, but unless we have a more specific understanding of how the principle is to be understood then this won't help us judge difficult cases, of which there are bound to be many. As it happens, proponents of sensitivity do have a quite sophisticated story to tell in this regard, but in order to understand this we first need to talk briefly about possible worlds.

Interlude: possible worlds

We are presently in the *actual world*. The actual world is simply how things are. Things might have been otherwise though. For example, although as it happens I am in fact sitting at my desk typing this chapter just how, things could have been different – I could, for instance, have been downstairs cooking dinner, or in another room playing with my sons. A useful philosophical device when it comes to thinking about these possible states of affairs is to imagine a *possible world*, one in which, for instance, everything is the same as the actual world except that I am downstairs cooking the dinner right now. This possible world is very much like the actual world, in that very little would have needed to have changed about the actual world in order to turn it into this possible world. Some possible worlds are very different to the actual world, however, such as the possible world in which, say, the fundamental laws of physics are different. We can thus 'order' possible worlds in terms of how similar they are to the actual world – i.e., in terms of how much is different from the actual world.

Possible worlds are particularly useful when considering counterfactual statements. Consider the following conditional claim that a military historian might be interested in: had Germany won the battle of Stalingrad, then they would have won World War Two. In the actual world, of course, Germany lost the battle of Stalingrad, and subsequently went on to lose World War Two. But it's not the actual world that we're interested in when we are evaluating the truth of this claim, but rather the closest possible world in which, contrary to what actually happened (this is what makes this claim a *counterfactual* statement), Germany won the battle of Stalingrad. A useful way of thinking about this is to imagine that you have God-like powers to control history. Using these powers, you press the 'rewind' button on history and go back to before the battle of Stalingrad. You now change whatever you need to change to ensure that Germany wins this battle, but nothing else. We now have the closest possible world in which Germany wins the battle of Stalingrad. Now you press the 'play' button on history and see what happens. If, in this possible world, Germany goes on to win World War Two, then this counterfactual claim is true. If, in contrast, it doesn't, then it is false.

As we will see, appealing to possible worlds in this way is very useful philosophically, which is why so many philosophers employ it. That such a notion is useful does not, however, make it legitimate, and there are some non-trivial worries about possible worlds. For example, when a statement about the actual world is true we have a fairly clear grip on what it is that makes it true – i.e., that it is some feature of the actual world. Clearly, though, we cannot straightforwardly apply this reasoning to statements involving possible worlds, since (intuitively at any rate) such worlds don't really exist. There are also worries about the objectivity of statements about possible worlds. After all, similarity is a very vague, and possibly even context-sensitive, notion, and so one might wonder whether there could not be a lot of variability in the truth-values that we intuitively attribute to statements about possible worlds. And there are other problems too.

Despite these difficulties, however, I think we can legitimately employ this framework without further concern for our purposes here. For one thing, it is often the case that when pursuing some area of philosophy one has to take as given answers to questions that are unresolved within another area of philosophy (for example, a lot of the discussion in ethics presupposes the possibility of free will, and yet this metaphysical issue is far from settled). Accordingly, it is not unusual that we have to help ourselves to a framework that is philosophically contentious outside of epistemology. Moreover, even if it were to turn out that possible worlds talk is unsustainable, this would not mean the end of the kind of epistemological approach sketched here. Instead, it would simply mean that we would have to re-cast this approach within a different framework. With these two points in mind, we will return to consider the sensitivity principle.

Back to sensitivity

Here's how possible world talk is very useful for our purposes. Consider again the sensitivity principle and, in particular, the phrase 'had p been false, then S would not have believed that p'. Obviously, since in the actual world p is both true and believed by S, we can't evaluate this statement by considering the actual world. It is thus a *modal* principle – i.e., a principle that implicitly appeals to modal notions like that of a possible world. Instead, the world we are interested in when we evaluate this statement is a possible world – i.e., a non-actual world where things are different to how they in fact are. Using the possible worlds framework, we can be more precise about which possible world is the relevant one. That is, the possible world we are interested in is the one where everything is the same except that which would need to be different for p to be false (i.e., the *closest* possible world in which p is false). The question we then need to ask is: what does our agent believe in this world? If she continues to believe p regardless, then her belief is insensitive; while if she no longer believes p, then her belief is sensitive.

Going back to the Roddy case, we can see the possible worlds framework in action. In the actual world Roddy believes that there is a sheep in the field (p) and there is a sheep in the field (i.e., p is true). In order to evaluate whether his belief is sensitive we now need to consider the closest possible world in which p is false – i.e., the world where as little else changes other than the truth of p. Such a world would be where everything is the same except that there is no sheep in the field. What does Roddy believe in this world? Well, clearly he will carry on believing that there is a sheep in the field regardless, since he will still be looking at the sheep-shaped big hairy dog in front of him. In contrast, had Roddy formed his belief by actually looking at a sheep, then this problem wouldn't arise. The nearest possible world in which p is false in this case would be a world in which the sheep that Roddy is looking at is no longer there. But if there is no sheep there, then he wouldn't believe that there is a sheep in the field and so his belief would be sensitive.

Given the elegant way in which the sensitivity condition deals with cases like this, one can see why one would want to advocate the sensitivity principle as a condition on knowledge in order to deal with the Gettier-style cases, and hence the Gettier problem.

Sensitivity and the lottery problem

Another advantage of the sensitivity principle is that it can deal with some other epistemological problems besides the Gettier problem. Most notable of these is the *lottery problem*, a problem which, like the Gettier problem, also appeals to the anti-luck intuition. Consider the following case:

> *Lottie*
> Lottie buys a lottery ticket for a fair lottery with very long odds. As it happens, Lottie has one of the losing tickets, but she has yet to hear what the result of the lottery was. Nevertheless, she reflects on the fact that the odds involved are so long and as a result forms the belief that she's lost. Consequently, she tears up her ticket without even bothering to check the results (e.g., in a reliable national newspaper).

I take it we have a very strong intuition that Lottie's behaviour here is irrational, and the reason for this is that she doesn't know that her ticket has lost. Here is the puzzle, though: why not? After all, the odds in favour of her belief are about as good as odds can ever be. Moreover, it is probably more likely that she should form a false belief by reading the result in a reliable national newspaper (because of a misprint, say), than that she should form a false belief by reflecting on the odds involved (this belief-forming process is almost guaranteed to be right). But why, then, can one come to know that one has lost the lottery by looking up the results in a reliable newspaper, and yet one cannot come to know this by merely reflecting on the astronomical odds involved in winning a lottery, even though the odds that one's belief is wrong based on the former basis are a lot higher than the odds that one's belief is wrong based on the latter basis? This is the lottery problem.

What the lottery problem seems to illustrate is that knowledge is not a straightforward function of the evidential probability in favour of your belief. That is, one might naturally think that whether or not one has knowledge is proportional to how likely it is that one's belief is true given one's evidence. What the lottery problem seems to show, however, is that this is not the case. After all, it is *more* likely that your belief is true if it is based solely on the evidence gained by considering the astronomical odds involved in winning a lottery than if it is based solely on the evidence gaining by reading the results in a reliable newspaper. And yet one gains knowledge in the latter case but not the former.

Proponents of the sensitivity principle have a straightforward explanation of why Lottie does not know. After all, even despite the strong probabilistic evidential support she has in favour of her belief, her belief is insensitive. In the nearest possible world in which she's won the lottery, and yet everything else stays the same, she will continue to believe that she's lost. This might initially seem puzzling, since how can the world in which Lottie wins the lottery be a *near-by* world, given that winning the lottery is such a low probability event? Remember, though, that the ordering of possible worlds is down to their *similarity* to the actual world, and the world in which a lottery ticket holder wins the lottery is a world just like the actual world – all that needs to be different is that a few coloured balls fall in a slightly different configuration. This highlights an important point: low probability events happen in possible worlds like the actual world. (This, by the way, is the point of the slogan for the British National Lottery: "It could be you!". The 'could' here is the 'could' of modal nearness, not the 'could' of probabilistic likelihood. After all, from a probabilistic point of view, it *couldn't* be you, as the odds are astronomically against you. But what is true is that if one plays the lottery, then there is a close possible world where one is a winner.)

In contrast, forming your belief in this case by reading the result in a reliable newspaper, even though the chance of error might be greater, *will* result in a sensitive belief. After all, in the nearest possible world in which one's belief is no longer true – i.e., where one wins the lottery – a reliable newspaper will print this result and so one's belief would change accordingly – one would believe that one has won the lottery. Sensitivity, then, generates just the right result: Lottie lacks knowledge, while her counterpart who reads the result in a newspaper has knowledge.

Methods

There is a complication to the sensitivity principle that we need to remark on at this juncture (it is a complication that will also apply to the safety principle that we are going to consider in a moment). So far, we have been evaluating whether a true belief is sensitive by simply considering the nearest possible worlds in which what the agent believes is false.

A little reflection reveals, however, that we need to be more specific about which worlds are relevant to this evaluation. In order to see this, consider the following example:

Granny
Granny is a grandmother who is very good at being able to tell whether her grandson is well provided that she gets to have a good look at him. One day her grandson visits and she gets a good look at him. She sees that he is well and so forms a belief to this effect. Had her grandson not been well, however, then his family, not wanting to worry Granny, would have kept her grandson away from her and told her that he was well regardless. Moreover, Granny would have believed them.

Intuitively, Granny does know that her grandson is well. After all, she gets a good look at him and in these cognitive conditions she is an excellent judge about his health. If, however, we evaluate whether her belief is sensitive by simply considering the nearest possible world in which what she believes is false (i.e., the world in which her grandson is unwell), then it will turn out that her belief is *in*sensitive, and thus that she lacks knowledge. After all, in this possible world, her grandson's family will keep the grandson away and lie to Granny about the state of his health. In this possible world, then, Granny will form a *false* belief about the target proposition. The sensitivity principle thus seems to generate the wrong result in this case.

Rather than abandon the sensitivity principle as a constraint on knowledge, the right response is to be a little more specific about which possible worlds are the relevant ones when it comes to evaluating whether a belief is sensitive. After all, in the Granny example just described, it seems that the possible world in which she forms her belief about the target proposition by listening to the *testimony* of her relatives is precisely the wrong possible world to evaluate whether her ability to spot whether her grandson is well *by looking* is good enough to produce knowledge. What is problematic about evaluating the sensitivity of her belief in this way is that we are evaluating the sensitivity of her belief, formed by getting a good look at her grandson, by considering what she believes in a possible world in which she employs an entirely *different* belief-forming method – i.e., listening to the testimony of her family. But why should the fact that the latter belief-forming method is unreliable mean that the belief-forming method that Granny actually uses is not knowledge-conducive?

What this case seems to demand, then, is that we need to relativize the sensitivity principle to the particular belief-forming method that is actually used. That is, the possible world that we need to consider in order to evaluate whether a belief is sensitive is the nearest possible world in which the target proposition is false and the agent forms a belief in that proposition using the same belief-forming method as in the actual world. In this way, the sensitivity principle will generate the right result in the Granny case. For while it remains true that the nearest possible world in which what she believes is false she continues to believe the target proposition regardless, this won't now be the relevant possible world to consider when evaluating whether her belief is sensitive. Instead, we will need to look at the nearest possible world in which what she believes is no longer true – i.e., her grandson is unwell – *and* she forms her belief about this proposition in the same way as in the actual world – i.e., by getting a good look at him. Crucially, however, in *this* world she will form the belief that her grandson is unwell, since she is *ex hypothesi* good at spotting if he is unwell by getting a good look at him. Hence, on this specification of the sensitivity principle, the grandmother has knowledge of the target proposition, just as intuition predicts. Since this refinement to our understanding of the sensitivity principle is well motivated, this speaks in favour of the sensitivity principle as a condition on knowledge.

One last point is in order on this topic. The talk here of belief-forming methods is apt to mislead. After all, a method is usually something one employs self-consciously. Crucially, however, this is not the meaning of 'method' that is in play here, since much of our knowledge does not result from a method in this sense at all (think, for example, of much of our perceptual knowledge). Rather, what is meant is merely whatever cognitive process gave rise to the belief, whether that process is self-consciously employed or not.

Formulating the anti-luck condition II: safety

There are, however, some problems with the sensitivity principle. We will examine two of these problems at a later juncture when we look at the issue of radical scepticism in chapter six, since this principle is often employed in this context. (In short, these problems are that: (i) the sensitivity principle may be incompatible with a fundamental epistemic principle, called the closure principle; and, relatedly, (ii) the sensitivity principle, at least when appropriately relativized to methods, may not be able to offer the response to scepticism that it advertises). One problem with the sensitivity principle that is important for our purposes is that it seems to disallow knowledge in some cases where, intuitively, knowledge is possessed. Consider the following case:

Ernie
Ernie lives in a high-rise block of flats in which the way to dispose of one's garbage is to drop it down a garbage chute in the corridor. Ernie knows that the flats are well maintained, and so when he drops his garbage down the chute he believes that it will soon be in the basement.

Intuitively, Ernie does know that the garbage is in the basement. After all, he knows that the flats are well maintained, and thus the possibility that it isn't in the basement is pretty remote. Nevertheless, his belief in this regard is insensitive, since in the closest possible world in which his belief is false – e.g., the world in which everything else stays the same but the garbage snags on the way down the chute – he would continue to believe that the garbage is in the basement. After all, Ernie hasn't seen the rubbish actually arrive in the basement. Notice, furthermore, that what goes for the rubbish chute case goes for lots of other cases as well. Indeed, it will go for pretty much any case of inductive knowledge – i.e., any case in which the agent forms her belief on a solid inductive basis and hence lacks first-hand knowledge of the truth of the target proposition. After all, what is important to the case is only that Ernie, while having excellent grounds to believe what he does, has not actually seen the rubbish in the basement, and so knows it merely inductively. Intuitively, however, we have lots of inductive knowledge of this sort, and yet if the sensitivity principle is a condition on knowledge then knowledge of this kind is rare, if not impossible.

It is cases like this that have led some commentators to argue that the right modal principle to adopt when it comes to eliminating knowledge-undermining epistemic luck is not the sensitivity principle but rather a different principle known as the *safety principle*. Roughly, the safety principle can be formulated as follows:

The Safety Principle
If S knows that p, then S's true belief that p is such that S's belief could not have easily been wrong.

Stated in terms of possible worlds, what this principle demands is not just that one's belief is true in the actual world, but that in all – or at least nearly all; there is some debate on this, as we will see in a moment – near-by possible worlds in which S continues to believe that p, her belief continues to be true. As with the sensitivity principle, this possible worlds specification needs to be relativized to the actual belief-forming method used by the agent. That is, the possible worlds that are relevant are those in which the agent continues to believe that p via the same belief-forming method used in the actual world.

This principle will handle Gettier-style cases. Consider the Roddy case, for example. While Roddy's belief is true in the actual world, there is a wide class of near-by possible worlds in which he forms a false belief – i.e., the possible worlds in which the sheep in question is no longer present, but where the sheep-shaped object is still in view. In such worlds, Roddy will form a false belief that the sheep is in the field. In general, when it comes to Gettier-style cases, the safety principle is just as effective as the sensitivity principle.

The safety principle can also handle the Ernie case. For notice that while Ernie's belief is insensitive, it is safe. After all, given that the flat is well maintained, there won't be a close possible world in which the bag snags. Accordingly, in all near-by possible worlds in which Ernie continues to believe that the rubbish is in the basement, his belief will be true. And what goes for the Ernie case will also apply to cases of inductive knowledge more generally.

Finally, the safety principle can also deal with the lottery problem, although this is a little more controversial. In order to see this, remember that lottery wins occur in near-by possible worlds. Accordingly, there will be a class of near-by possible worlds in which Lottie continues to believe the target proposition (that she has lost the lottery) via the same belief-forming method (considering the odds involved) and yet forms a false belief. This point can often be lost because it is natural to think of the possible world in which one wins the lottery as a far-off possible world. However, as we noted above, low probability events can obtain in near-by possible worlds, since possible worlds are ordered not in terms of probability but in terms of similarity. Accordingly, there is no problem in the idea that these worlds are close worlds and hence as being able to undermine the safety of a belief.

Nonetheless, there is an important issue here that we should highlight. So far we have talked rather vaguely about safety requiring that one's true belief remain true across all, or at least nearly all, near-by possible worlds. But which is it: all, or just nearly all? The worry is that if we are to deal with the lottery problem then we it seems we will need to opt for the former, more demanding, reading of the safety principle, but that this alternative will not then be able to accommodate other cases that we want this principle to deal with.

The reason why we seem to need to go for the stronger reading of the safety principle in order to deal with the lottery problem is that intuitively there are in fact very few possible worlds in which Lottie forms a false belief via the relevant belief-forming process. If we go for the weaker reading, then the worry will be that Lottie will count as having knowledge after all, contrary to intuition. But if one responds by opting for the stronger reading, then that might seem to deny knowledge to agents who intuitively do know. Consider the Ernie case again, for example. Given how Ernie forms his belief, surely there are some near-by possible worlds in which he forms a false belief on this basis? We thus seem to be caught in a dilemma, in that if we strengthen the safety principle then we deal with the lottery problem at the expense of being unable to accommodate other cases; while if we weaken the safety principle then we can accommodate these other cases but now cannot deal with the lottery problem.

This is a genuine problem, but it is far from fatal to the view. In particular, there are two ways for the proponent of the safety principle to go here. The first simply involves a defence of the strong reading. Consider again the Ernie case that we just noted could pose a problem for the strong reading of the safety principle. In order to pose this problem, it is essential that there be near-by possible worlds in which Ernie forms a false belief that his garbage is in the basement, where his belief is formed on the same basis as in the actual world. On closer inspection, however, it is far from obvious that there are any near-by possible worlds which fulfil this remit, at least insofar as Ernie has knowledge. Imagine for a moment that there are near-by possible worlds where the rubbish does not make it to the basement. That would mean, for example, there is something amiss with the garbage chute itself, such as an imperfection in the shaft that rubbish could very easily snag on. But if that's true, then surely it isn't at all intuitive that Ernie has knowledge in this case, since clearly he could very easily be mistaken. Thus, the proponent of the strong reading of the safety principle could argue that insofar as there are near-by possible worlds in which the agent forms a false belief on the same basis as in the actual world, then that simply means that this agent doesn't have knowledge.

While I think that this line of response is defensible, I think there is a better proposal waiting in the wings. In order to see how this proposal works, we first need to consider a further motivation for the safety principle.

Anti-luck epistemology reconsidered

So far we have described an anti-luck epistemology as being any epistemology that motivates an epistemic condition on knowledge in terms of its ability to accommodate the anti-luck intuition. There is, however, a more substantive way of thinking about what an anti-luck epistemology involves. In particular, one might motivate such a proposal by explicitly analysing luck itself and then combining this with an account of the specific sense in which *bona fide* knowledge excludes luck. By putting these two components together, the idea is that one can potentially cast light on the nature of knowledge. Where this approach differs from proposals that simply argue for the safety or sensitivity principle is that such proposals typically take luck as a primitive notion and do not attempt to offer an analysis of it. If, however, what we are looking for is a way of eliminating luck from knowledge, then it could well be that understanding more about luck will have a bearing on how we should conceive of an anti-luck epistemology.

Interestingly, despite its central importance to many fundamental philosophical issues – for example, the problem of free will or the nature of causation, not to mention our current concern, which is the analysis of knowledge – there has been very little written by philosophers on luck. This is now starting to change, however. One recent proposal – what is known as the *modal account of luck* – argues that a lucky event is an event that obtains in the actual world but which does not obtain in a wide class of near-by possible worlds. So, for example, that the sun rose this morning is not a lucky event, since it obtains not just in the actual world but also in all near-by possible worlds. Winning the lottery, in contrast, is a lucky event since while it happens in the actual world there are lots of near-by possible worlds where this event doesn't occur.

There are a number of complexities to the modal account of luck, but we will restrict ourselves to just two of them here (the ones that are most salient for our purposes). The first is that we need to restrict the class of relevant possible worlds to those where the initial conditions for the target event are the same as in the actual world. We can see why this is important by considering the case of a lottery win. After all, that one does not win the lottery in near-by possible worlds in which one fails to buy a lottery ticket obviously has no bearing at all on the luckiness of your lottery win in the actual world. Instead, it is the fact that in most near-by possible worlds in which one buys a lottery ticket one fails to win the lottery which is relevant to the luckiness of your actual lottery win.

The second complexity that we need to note is that on this view luck will come in degrees depending on how close the near-by possible world is in which the target event doesn't obtain. We can illustrate this point in terms of the following example. Suppose that a sniper takes a shot at you in a warzone and the bullet misses your head by a few millimetres. Clearly, you are very lucky to be alive, and we can account for this on this view by noting that while you are alive in the actual world, there is a wide class of near-by possible worlds in which the relevant initial conditions for the target event obtain (e.g., someone takes a shot at you) and you are dead just now. Suppose, however, that the sniper's bullet missed you by more than a few millimetres; by a metre, say. Intuitively, it is still a matter of luck that you are alive, and again the account of luck on offer can accommodate this intuition since there is indeed still a wide class of relevant near-by possible worlds in which you are killed by this bullet. Nevertheless, what is also true is that you are *luckier* to be alive in the former case than in the latter case, and we can also account for that in terms of this analysis of luck. For what differentiates these two lucky events is that in the luckier of the two events the near-by possible world in which one is killed is closest. More generally, the closer the near-by possible world in which the target event obtains, the luckier the event will be.

As we will see, these two elements of the view are very important once we spell out the epistemological ramifications of the view. First, though, what sort of anti-luck epistemology does the modal account of luck favour? Well, it seems to favour those anti-luck accounts that incorporate the safety principle. Recall that we want to capture the sense in which, when one has knowledge, one has a true belief that is not true as a matter of luck. But what would it mean, on the modal account of luck, for one's true belief to be true as a matter of luck? Well, it would need to be the case that one's belief is true in the actual world, but false in close possible worlds. But it is precisely this eventuality that the safety principle excludes, in that it demands true belief not just in the actual world but also in close possible worlds. Safety is thus plausibly the anti-luck condition on knowledge.

A fully-fledged anti-luck epistemology – i.e., one that appeals to an account of luck – thus offers us a further basis for preferring the safety principle over the sensitivity principle, since only the former accords with the prior theory of luck. Going back to the complexities in the modal account of luck that we just noted, two more points are relevant here. The first is that the fact that this theory of luck only treats near-by possible worlds as relevant insofar as they share the relevant initial conditions of the target event conforms to the point noted earlier about how these modal principles need to be relativized to a method. For the process that gave rise to the belief is in effect the analogue of the 'relevant initial conditions' that we discussed as part of the modal account of luck. Just as when it comes to lucky events we are only interested in those possible worlds which share the relevant initial conditions with the target event, so when it comes to the issue of whether a belief is only luckily true we are only interested in those possible worlds in which the belief-forming process is the same as in the actual world.

The second complexity we noted, regarding how the modal theory of luck can account for how some lucky events are luckier than others, is important because it offers us a second way out of the problem we posed for the safety principle at the end of the last section. Recall that this problem had the form of a dilemma. On the one hand, if we interpret the safety principle robustly – such that we consider *all* near-by possible worlds where one forms a belief in the target proposition on the same basis as in the actual world – then it seems that we can deal with the lottery problem at the expense of being unable to explain why agents have knowledge in other cases, such as the Ernie case. On the other hand, if we interpret the safety principle in a weaker fashion – such that we only consider *nearly all* near-by possible worlds where one forms a belief in the target proposition on the same basis as in the actual world – then we can deal with cases like the Ernie case but at the expense of now being unable to respond to the lottery problem. We noted above that the strong reading of the safety principle is probably more defensible on this score than it might at first appear. Interestingly, however, once the modal account of luck is plugged into one's anti-luck epistemology, it may give us an even better way out of this problem.

The crux of the matter is that when it comes to evaluations of whether an event is lucky, not all the near-by possible worlds are on a par. Instead, those near-by possible worlds that are closer to the actual world – i.e., which are most similar to the actual world – carry more weight in our evaluations of whether an event is lucky than those near-by possible worlds which are less close. In order to see this, just consider the example given above of the person narrowly avoiding being shot. That one was nearly killed by a bullet that passed by a few millimetres away is one thing; that one was nearly killed by a bullet that passed by a metre away something else. Both events are lucky, but the former is luckier than the latter. The same goes for knowledge. For while it may well be the case that in the Ernie case and the Lottie case there is roughly the same proportion of near-by possible worlds in which the agent forms a false belief in the target proposition, this doesn't suffice to show that both beliefs are equally safe. What is also relevant is how close these near-by possible worlds are. In this way, the proponent of the safety principle can argue that the near-by possible worlds should be *weighed*, in the sense that a false belief in the target proposition in the very near near-by possible worlds should count for more than a false belief in the target proposition in not so very near near-by possible worlds. Since in the Lottie case the relevant possible worlds in which she forms a false belief in the target proposition are very close – and certainly much closer than in the Ernie case – this can explain why the agent lacks knowledge in the one case but possesses it in the other.

A useful way of thinking about this point is in terms of *risk*. Having a bullet narrowly miss you is riskier than having the bullet pass you by a metre away. Applied to the epistemic case, the risk of a false belief in the lottery case is much higher, since it is modally closer, than in the Ernie case, and this has a bearing on our willingness to attribute knowledge. What we have is thus a *continuum* of epistemic risk. Where the risk is modally very close, as in the lottery case, then we do not attribute knowledge because the risk of error, and thus the luck involved in having a true belief, is too high. Where the risk is very far-off, in contrast, then we are inclined to attribute knowledge, since there is no serious risk of error, and relatedly no luck involved in having a true belief either. Between these two extremes there is a sliding scale of epistemic risk, where at some point – in all likelihood an indeterminate range – our inclination not to attribute knowledge stops and we start to attribute knowledge. The point is that we need to understand the safety principle such that it accommodates this idea of a continuum of epistemic risk, and the modal account of luck that underpins it.

In summary, we have noted that the safety principle has a number of advantages over the sensitivity principle. Moreover, the safety principle seems to be motivated by a fully-fledged anti-luck epistemology – i.e., an epistemology that is explicitly motivated in terms of an analysis of luck.

Robust anti-luck epistemology

Given the foregoing, one might naturally wonder whether it might be possible to completely analyse knowledge in terms of a true belief that satisfies the relevant anti-luck condition (i.e., the safety principle, it would seem). That is, one might think that knowledge just is non-lucky true belief, and hence that the analysis of knowledge is very straightforward: knowledge is just safe true belief. This would be a version of robust anti-luck epistemology.

Robust anti-luck epistemology is clearly an externalist account of knowledge, since the safety principle is itself an external epistemic condition and there is no other epistemic condition demanded, internal or otherwise. Modest anti-luck epistemology, in contrast, could be an internalist account of knowledge, depending on whether it insisted, over and above the anti-luck condition (the safety principle) on an internal epistemic condition, such as the justification condition, classically conceived. If one is already attracted to epistemic internalism, then one will ultimately not be inclined to endorse robust anti-luck epistemology. Still, even epistemic internalists should be able to concede that robust anti-luck epistemology has some attractions.

Recall the two over-arching intuitions about knowledge that we noted in chapter one – the ability and the anti-luck intuition. Robust anti-luck epistemology in effect treats the anti-luck intuition as the dominant intuition and so holds that one can account for the ability intuition in terms of the anti-luck condition that is designed to accommodate the anti-luck intuition. As we have seen, there is some plausibility in this suggestion, since the anti-luck condition – which we are taking to be the safety principle – can deal with a range of cases in epistemology. Moreover, since these cases include cases of knowledge that meet the ability intuition, there is something to the idea that the safety principle can accommodate the ability intuition. For example, the knowledge possessed in the Ernie case clearly involves a true belief that is the product of the agent's cognitive ability, and we have noted that because this belief is safe the safety-based account of knowledge can explain why knowledge is possessed in this case.

If robust anti-luck epistemology can accommodate both the anti-luck and the ability intuitions, however, then there is every reason to think that it would be a fully adequate theory of knowledge, in the sense that it can deal with every kind of case that we would want it to deal with. Moreover, it would also be an extremely elegant proposal. In short, there would be a lot to commend it. Unfortunately, however, on closer inspection it turns out that the view faces some pretty formidable obstacles. I here review two.

Problems with robust anti-luck epistemology I: necessary propositions

One issue that faces robust anti-luck epistemology is how to deal with knowledge of necessary propositions. Since these are propositions that are true in all near-by possible worlds, they are not easily accommodated by the safety principle as it presently stands. Consider the following case:

Mathema
Mathema uses a calculator to find out what 12 × 13 is equal to. As a result, he forms a true belief that 12 × 13 = 156. Unbeknownst to Mathema, however, his calculator is in fact broken and is simply generating answers at random. It is pure chance, then, that Mathema has formed a true belief in this proposition.

Notice that Mathema's belief is not only true but also (apparently) safe, even despite being formed in what is clearly an epistemically deficient fashion. For given that there is no possible world in which this proposition is false then, *a fortiori*, there is no near-by possible world in which Mathema falsely believes this proposition. Clearly, though, Mathema does not have knowledge of this proposition, given how his belief was formed. One cannot gain knowledge of an arithmetical truth by using a broken calculator.

Does this mean that robust anti-luck epistemology is essentially flawed, in that it cannot deal with knowledge more generally, as opposed to simply knowledge of a specific type (i.e., knowledge of contingent propositions)? Not at all. Recall that the general idea behind the safety principle – indeed, behind anti-luck epistemology more generally – is that knowledge entails a true belief that could not have easily been false.

The Safety Principle
If S knows that p, then S's true belief that p is such that S's belief could not have easily been false.

This principle is naturally glossed, however, by saying that knowledge entails a true belief *that p* which could not have easily been false. We thus get this more restrictive formulation of the safety principle:

The Restricted Safety Principle
If S knows that p, then S's true belief that p is such that S's belief *that p* could not have easily been false.

That is, the gloss demands that the agent not have a false belief *that p* in the relevant near-by possible worlds. Crucially, however, there is a sense in which a belief could very easily have been false even though there is no relevant near-by possible world in which the agent forms a false belief in the same proposition.

In order to see this, consider again the case just described. Intuitively, given how Mathema formed her belief that 12 × 13 = 156, it *could* very easily have been false, even though there is no near-by possible world in which this proposition is false (and hence, *a fortiori*, no relevant near-by possible world in which Mathema has a false belief). There are, after all, near-by possible worlds in which Mathema forms a mathematical belief in the same way as in the actual world (i.e., by using the faulty calculator) and ends up with a false belief even if there is no near-by possible world in which he uses this belief-forming method to do the impossible feat of forming a false belief that 12 × 13 = 156. Consider, for example, the near-by possible world in which Mathema uses his faulty calculator and ends up forming a false belief that 12 × 13 = 152.

One way of putting this point is that the safety principle, properly understood at any rate, is concerned not with the safety of a belief *that p* (i.e., the proposition actually believed), but rather with the safety of a relevant doxastic output of a belief-forming process (which, while resulting in a belief that p in the actual world, could result in a belief in a different proposition in a near-by possible world). In this way, possible worlds where this process results in a different doxastic output from that which results in the actual world – such as a belief that q rather than that p – can be relevant to the safety of the belief. On the face of it at least, this modification of the view enables it to deal with cases involving necessary propositions. Moreover, since this more general formulation is meant to best capture the key thought underlying the safety principle (and thus the anti-luck intuition too), there ought not to be any concern that this is an *ad hoc* way of dealing with this problem.

One worry about reading the safety principle in this way is that it introduces a new layer of vagueness regarding which possible worlds are relevant when it comes to determining whether a belief is safe. After all, one advantage of the narrower formulation of the safety principle is that at least it is clear on this formulation that it is only those near-by possible worlds in which the agent continues to form a belief that p which are in the market to be counted as relevant to whether or not the target belief is safe. In contrast, on the more inclusive formulation of the safety principle a much wider range of near-by possible worlds are potentially relevant, and thus the proper delineation of the salient possible worlds will be that much harder.

Even setting this concern to one side, there is a more fundamental difficulty waiting in the wings for the safety principle, even on the more general formulation. In order to see this, we only need to imagine an adapted version of the Mathema case:

Mathemi
Mathemi uses a calculator to find out what 12 × 13 is equal to. As a result, she forms a true belief that 12 × 13 = 156. Unbeknownst to Mathemi, however, her calculator is in fact malfunctioning. In particular, the calculator has two faults, albeit two faults that systematically cancel each other out when it comes to calculations within a given range, one that Mathemi's calculation falls well within.

Intuitively, given the faults in Mathemi's calculator she cannot gain knowledge that 12 × 13 = 156 in this way. As with the Mathema case, her belief is safe in the sense that she has a belief that could not have easily been false – there are no near-by possible worlds in which Mathemi forms a false belief that 12 × 13 = 156. Her belief thus satisfies the restricted safety principle. Interestingly, however, her belief also satisfies the more general formulation of the safety principle too, and hence we cannot appeal to the distinction between the general and restrictive formulations of this principle to account for this case. For notice that given that her calculator is malfunctioning in a way such that its two faults will cancel out each other as regards calculations of the sort that Mathemi is conducting, it follows that in all near-by possible worlds in which Mathemi forms her beliefs about mathematical claims of this sort by using this calculator, her beliefs will continue to be true.

It's not clear how robust anti-luck epistemology could adapt itself to deal with cases like Mathemi, and thus they pose a pretty severe problem for the view, at least insofar as the view is meant to apply to knowledge of all propositions, and not just contingent propositions.

Problems with robust anti-luck epistemology II: the Temp case

It is worth noting what the underlying problem posed by the Mathemi case is. For basically what it reveals is that an agent can have a belief in a necessary proposition which exhibits the right kind of modal stability to satisfy the anti-luck condition – i.e., the safety principle, whichever way it is formulated – and yet which is not sufficiently due to the agent's cognitive ability to qualify as knowledge (but is rather more the result of some environmental quirk). In short, as regards knowledge of some necessary propositions at least, robust anti-luck epistemology cannot accommodate the ability intuition. Interestingly, this is not a problem that is restricted to knowledge of necessary propositions, but in fact infects the robust anti-luck account of knowledge in general. If that is right, then the robust anti-luck epistemologist is wrong to treat the anti-luck intuition as the dominant intuition, since in fact there will be no formulation of the anti-luck condition that could adequately answer to the ability intuition.

Consider the following example:

Temp
Temp's job is to keep a record of the temperature in the room that he is in. He does this by consulting a thermometer on the wall. As it happens, this way of forming his beliefs about the temperature in the room will always result in a true belief. The reason for this, however, is not because the thermometer is working properly, since in fact it isn't – it is fluctuating randomly within a given range. Crucially, however, there is someone hidden in the room next to the thermostat who, unbeknownst to Temp, makes sure that every time Temp consults the thermometer the temperature in the room is adjusted so that it corresponds to the reading on the thermometer.

Clearly Temp cannot gain knowledge of the temperature of the room by consulting a broken thermometer. Interestingly, however, given how the example is set up, there is nothing that would prevent Temp's beliefs, so formed, from being safe.

After all, that there happens to be someone who is adjusting the thermostat to ensure that reading the broken thermometer always gives Temp a true belief need not be just an incidental fact about the example but could well be replicated in all near-by possible worlds. Perhaps, for example, the helper has some strong motivation to play this role – his life depends on it, say – and the actual world is such that there is nothing that could easily stand in his way in this regard (e.g., there's no scope for something to easily prevent him from changing the dial on the thermostat, or for the thermostat to stop working, or for the helper to be unable to observe the reading on the thermometer, etc.). Once we spell out the example in this way, however, then it ought to start to become clear what problem it poses for robust anti-luck epistemology. For if the helper is performing his role in all near-by possible worlds, then the target true belief will be safe and hence will meet the anti-luck condition on knowledge. That is, there will be no near-by possible world in which Temp forms his belief in the target proposition on the same basis as in the actual world and yet ends up with a false belief (nor, for that matter, will there be a near-by possible world where he employs the same belief-forming process and yet ends up with a false belief, whether in the target proposition or in a related proposition). His belief is therefore safe, and hence should count as knowledge by the lights of a robust anti-luck epistemology.

And yet this clearly isn't a case of knowledge. But if the reason why this case is not an instance of knowledge need not involve a failure to satisfy the anti-luck intuition, then what is the problem here? Well, notice that the direction of fit between belief and fact in this case is all wrong. What we want in a case of knowledge is for one's beliefs to be responsive to the facts. In this case, however, the direction of fit is entirely in reverse, since the facts are in effect responding to the agent's beliefs rather than *vice versa*. In particular, what has gone wrong in this case is that Temp's true belief is not sufficiently creditable to his cognitive agency, but is instead more due to some feature of the situation that is completely unconnected with his cognitive agency (i.e., the intervention of the helper). But this means that while this belief satisfies the anti-luck intuition, it does not satisfy the ability intuition. In short, while Temp's beliefs aren't luckily true – in fact, they are *guaranteed* to be true – this doesn't in any substantive way reflect his cognitive agency, but is rather attributable to the external intervention of the hidden helper.

Concluding remarks

In a nutshell, then, the problem facing robust anti-luck epistemology is that it cannot completely accommodate the ability intuition. Of course, one option here is to insist that robust anti-luck epistemology accounts for this intuition to the degree that it should account for it, and argue on this basis that cases like the Temp case should be thought of as involving genuine instances of knowledge. While such a stance is not without its theoretical attractions – robust anti-luck epistemology represents a very simple view of knowledge after all, one that can handle lots of different cases very well – the strong pull of the ability intuition makes such a stance very unattractive.

But if robust anti-luck epistemology is unable to accommodate the ability intuition, then that means that we need to look elsewhere to find an adequate theory of knowledge. In particular, it behoves us to take seriously those theories of knowledge that take the accommodation of the ability intuition as being central. It is to these views that we will now turn.

Chapter summary

In this chapter we have looked more closely at *anti-luck epistemology*, which is an approach to the theory of knowledge which focuses on finding the epistemic condition that would accommodate the anti-luck intuition (i.e., the *anti-luck epistemic condition*). Anti-luck epistemology comes in a robust and modest version. According to *robust anti-luck epistemology*, knowledge is nothing more than true belief that satisfies the anti-luck condition. According to *modest anti-luck epistemology*, while the anti-luck condition is necessary for knowledge, it won't be sufficient (with true belief) for knowledge. Robust anti-luck epistemology is a form of epistemic externalism about knowledge, while modest anti-luck epistemology is compatible with epistemic internalism about knowledge. One candidate for the anti-luck condition is the *sensitivity principle*. This demands, roughly, that one has a true belief such that, had what one believed been false, one wouldn't have believed it. We saw that principles like this are best understood in terms of the language of *possible worlds*. It is also important that they are relativized to *methods*. While the sensitivity principle fares well in explaining why we lack knowledge in Gettier-style and lottery cases, it struggles to account for inductive knowledge. This led us to explore a different prospective anti-luck condition, known as the *safety principle*. This demands, roughly, that one has a true belief that could not have easily been wrong. Like the sensitivity principle, the safety principle can also deal with Gettier-style and lottery cases. Unlike the sensitivity principle, however, it can also account for inductive knowledge. There were some issues about the correct formulation of safety that arose at this juncture, however, and to resolve them we explored a more fully-fledged notion of anti-luck epistemology. This proceeded by offering a theory of luck and then on this basis motivating a particular anti-luck epistemic condition. To this end, the *modal account of luck* was outlined, and it was shown how this motivated not just the safety principle in general, but also a specific rendering of the safety principle which in effect 'weighted' possible worlds in terms of how close they are to the actual world. The prospects for robust anti-luck epistemology in light of this account were then explored. One problem facing this proposal, concerning our knowledge of necessary propositions, was found to be illusory, in that it traded on a faulty rendering of the safety principle. But a deeper problem emerged, which related to the fact that a belief could be radically immune to knowledge-undermining epistemic luck and yet fail to qualify as knowledge because this cognitive success is in no way significantly attributable to the subject's cognitive agency. In short, there are cases of belief which satisfy the anti-luck intuition, but which do not satisfy the ability intuition.

Further introductory reading

For a recent critical exchange regarding the anti-luck condition on knowledge, see Hetherington (2014) and Pritchard (2014c). For a fairly accessible discussion of the relative merits of safety, sensitivity, and the notion of an anti-luck epistemology, see Pritchard (2008). See also Black (2011). Becker (2013) offers a helpful annotated bibliography on modal epistemology. See also Engel (2011), which is also listed below under 'free internet resources'.

Further advanced reading

The classic defences of the sensitivity principle can be found in Dretske (1970) and Nozick (1981). For more on possible worlds, see Loux (1979). For some important recent discussions of the lottery problem, see Lewis (1996), Cohen (1998) and Williamson (2000, ch. 11). The Granny case is due to Nozick (1981, 179). The Ernie case is due to Sosa (2000), in which he also defends the safety principle. See also Sosa (1999). A clear statement of the objection that the safety principle cannot deal with the lottery problem can be found in Greco (2007). See Pritchard (2007*a*) for a response. For a recent defence of the modal account of luck, see Pritchard (2014b; cf. Pritchard 2005, ch. 5). For a recent collection of discussions of the philosophy of luck, see Pritchard & Whittington (2015). For some of the main works on anti-luck epistemology, see Pritchard (2005; 2007*a*; 2015a). An important precursor to anti-luck epistemology can be found in Unger (1968).

Free internet resources

For a helpful overview of the topic of epistemic luck, see Engel (2011). For more on the general issue of the analysis of knowledge, see Ichikawa & Steup (2012) and Hetherington (2015).

Study questions

1 Explain, in your own words, how the Gettier problem trades on the anti-luck intuition. Give an example to support your case.
2 What is the distinction between robust and modest anti-luck epistemology? Why is only robust anti-luck epistemology committed to epistemic externalism about knowledge?

3 What is the sensitivity principle, and how does it explain why we lack knowledge in Gettier-style and lottery cases?
4 Why does the sensitivity principle struggle to accommodate cases of inductive knowledge? Try to give your own example to support your case.
5 What are possible worlds, and how do they help us to make sense of modal principles like sensitivity and safety?
6 Why is it important to relativize modal principles like sensitivity and safety to the method actually employed? Try to give your own example to support your case.
7 What is the safety principle, and why is better placed to account for inductive knowledge than the sensitivity principle?
8 What is the modal account of luck, and how is it used to motivate the safety principle?
9 How must we understand the safety principle in order to account for our knowledge of necessary propositions?
10 Why is the Temp case alleged to show that robust anti-luck epistemology is untenable? Do you find it persuasive? If not, why not?

Sample essay questions

1 'In order to solve the Gettier problem, we first need to offer a theory of luck.' Discuss.
2 Does knowledge entail safety or sensitivity (or neither)? Defend your answer.
3 Is it possible for one's beliefs to be completely immune to knowledge-undermining epistemic luck and yet in no significant way manifest one's cognitive agency? Insofar as this is possible, does this demonstrate that robust anti-luck epistemology is untenable as a theory of knowledge?

3
Virtue Epistemology

Problems for process reliabilism

In chapter 1 we encountered a simple form of reliabilism about knowledge, called *process reliabilism*. This held that knowledge is true belief that is formed via a reliable process, where a reliable process is one that tends to lead to true beliefs rather than false beliefs. We noted that process reliabilism cannot deal with Gettier-style cases, and hence that it cannot be a fully adequate account of knowledge, at least as it stands. Given that Gettier-style cases essentially trade on the anti-luck intuition – the intuition that knowledge involves a true belief that couldn't have easily been wrong – it follows that process reliabilism cannot accommodate this platitude about knowledge.

There are some other problems facing process reliabilism. One of these problems (we will consider some others in the next section) is particularly fundamental, in that the view seems unable to capture the sense in which genuine knowledge reflects a responsiveness on one's part to the facts. In order to see this, consider again the Temp case described at the end of chapter 2. What is not in question in this case is that Temp is forming his beliefs in a way such that they will tend to be true. On the face of it, then, Temp's belief-forming process is reliable and hence he should be able to gain knowledge by forming his beliefs in this way, at least if process reliabilism is true. Temp clearly does not have knowledge, however, and the reason for this, as we noted in chapter 2, is that there is the wrong direction of fit between his beliefs and the facts. What we want in a case of knowledge is a belief that is responsive to the facts; but what we have in this case is, in effect, a situation in which the facts are being responsive to what Temp believes. In short, the truth of Temp's beliefs are not sufficiently the result of his cognitive agency (but rather due to the external intervention of the hidden helper), and that means that they do not satisfy the ability intuition (i.e., the intuition that knowledge involves a true belief that is the product of the agent's cognitive ability).

Process reliabilism is thus unable to accommodate the ability intuition, and given how fundamental this intuition is to our thinking about knowledge, this is a pretty decisive strike against the view, especially given that it is likewise unable to accommodate the anti-luck intuition as well.

From process reliabilism to virtue epistemology

Interestingly, however, in the wake of the problems facing process reliabilism, a new form of reliabilism was proposed which could, it seems, at least accommodate the ability intuition. This view is known as *virtue reliabilism*, and it is a form of *virtue epistemology*. Just as virtue theories in ethics focus on the morally virtuous agent – the person who has the right mix of virtuous moral traits, and so should be admired and emulated – so virtue epistemological views focus on the mix of cognitive traits that one should possess in order to be a 'good' epistemic subject. What is common to all virtue epistemological accounts of knowledge is that they define knowledge in terms of the agent's reliable cognitive abilities, such as her faculties (e.g., her senses) and her intellectual virtues (e.g., her conscientiousness when dealing with evidence). Virtue reliabilism is one variant of this view (we will consider others in a moment), which essentially just remodels simple process reliabilism along virtue epistemic lines.

Here is how virtue reliabilism is usually formulated:

Virtue Reliabilism
S knows that *p* if and only if S's true belief that *p* is the product of the reliable cognitive abilities that make up her cognitive character.

Notice that just as with process reliabilism, the demand that agents form their beliefs in a reliable way is central to the proposal. Nevertheless, what is key to virtue reliabilism is that it places a restriction on which reliable processes count as knowledge-conducive. In particular, it is only those reliable processes that form part of the cognitive abilities that make up one's cognitive character.

In order to see what this restriction amounts to, consider again the Temp case. Here we have an agent who forms his belief in a reliable fashion but who lacks knowledge because the reliability in question does not reflect any responsiveness on his part to the facts. In short, the reason why his belief is true and reliably formed has little to do with his cognitive abilities (but everything to do with the intervention of the hidden helper). Virtue reliabilism can deal with cases like this, since it precisely isn't true of Temp that his true belief is a product of his reliable cognitive abilities (even though it is reliably formed). Instead, it is the product of environmental factors that are entirely independent of Temp's cognitive abilities (i.e., the intervention of the hidden helper). So far, then, so good.

Virtue reliabilism can also deal with some other problem cases that beset process reliabilism. Consider the following example:

Alvin
Alvin has a brain lesion. An odd fact about Alvin's brain lesion, however, is that it causes the sufferer to form the (true) belief that he has a brain lesion. Accordingly, Alvin truly believes that he has a brain lesion.

What's interesting about this case is that the way in which Alvin is forming his belief is certainly reliable. According to process reliabilism, then, it seems that Alvin ought to be able to gain knowledge that he has a brain lesion by forming his belief in this way. Nevertheless, we have a strong intuition that one can't gain knowledge in this manner. Virtue reliabilism offers an excellent explanation as to why – *viz.*, the belief-forming process in question is, intuitively, not a cognitive ability on the part of the agent.

We haven't yet said exactly what a cognitive ability is, except to give some examples. As just noted, intuitively the way in which the belief is being formed in the brain lesion case is not a cognitive ability, but one might argue that this just reflects an unprincipled conception of cognitive abilities. After all, if one is willing to allow one's basic sensory faculties to count as cognitive abilities as virtue reliabilists do, then why can't the reliable belief-forming process at issue in the Alvin case – which is, after all, a belief-forming process that takes place in the brain of the subject – count as a cognitive ability too? This is the point at which the appeal to cognitive character in the account of virtue reliabilism becomes important. For not just any reliable belief-forming trait qualifies as a cognitive ability. Instead, it is only those belief-forming traits which are appropriately integrated with one's other cognitive abilities, where the integrated whole is what constitutes one's cognitive character.

This seems right, since the point of virtue reliabilism is to capture the idea that the truth of your belief is down to *your* cognitive character. Yet if the relevant cognitive ability is not integrated within one's cognitive character in this way, then it is hard to see why we would regard your true belief as being in any way creditable to you.

Now there is an issue here of just how integrated a cognitive ability has to be within the agent's cognitive character before it counts as knowledge-conducive, but all will surely agree that the belief-forming process in play in the Alvin case is not integrated within the agent's cognitive character at all, and thus we have a good explanation of why simply reliably forming a true belief, even where the process is in some (attenuated) sense an 'internal' one, does not suffice for knowledge. Indeed, the natural thing to say about the Alvin case is that Alvin's belief is true *in spite of* his cognitive character (it is, after all, a kind of cognitive *malfunction*).

Interestingly, notice that if the belief-forming process in the Alvin case were to become appropriately integrated within Alvin's cognitive character, then it would start to become far more plausible to regard this trait as knowledge-conducive. For example, suppose that Alvin were to read in a medical journal about how there is a brain lesion that causes the sufferer to believe that he has a brain lesion. Given that he recalls simply finding himself with this belief one day, he now has good *prima facie* grounds to wonder whether he is suffering from this condition. Suppose further that he has managed to discount every other potential reason why he might believe this. Does his true belief now amount to knowledge? Admittedly, it isn't clear, but surely it is far less intuitive that this isn't knowledge than it was before, and the reason for this is surely that Alvin's cognitive traits are 'pulling together' to form a judgement in this regard, thereby integrating this particular belief-forming process within his cognitive character.

Virtue reliabilism versus virtue responsibilism

Virtue reliabilists, like reliabilists more generally, are epistemic externalists in that they don't think that an internal epistemic condition, like a justification condition, is necessary for knowledge. Indeed, virtue reliabilists often argue that their view is much better at accommodating internalist intuitions than other externalist views precisely because of how central the notion of cognitive character is to their position. That is, one might think that the key thought underlying epistemic internalism is that when an agent has knowledge she ought to be able to be cognitively responsible for what she believes. Internalists accommodate this thought by appealing to some sort of justification condition (i.e., by appealing to reflectively accessible supporting reasons), but virtue reliabilists argue that we can just as well accommodate it by appealing to the notion of cognitive character. According to virtue reliabilism, when one knows one is being held cognitively responsible for what one believes, in a sense at least, because it is down to one's own cognitive character that one's belief is true. So, for example, there is a straightforward sense in which the chicken-sexer Chuck, whom we encountered in chapter 1, is in a position to have knowledge on this view, because even though his beliefs lacks a justification, they are nonetheless formed as a result of his reliable cognitive abilities.

Still, some virtue epistemologists are not convinced by this move, and so offer an epistemic internalist version of virtue epistemology. Typically, such an internalist virtue epistemology – sometimes known as *virtue responsibilism* – argues that merely forming a belief as a result of one's reliable cognitive faculties does not suffice for knowledge. Instead, what is required is that the agent bring to bear one of her *intellectual virtues*. That is, whereas virtue reliabilists think that knowledge arises out of one's reliable cognitive faculties and intellectual virtues, virtue responsibilists tend to think that only the latter are knowledge-conducive.

One reason why you might think virtue responsibilism is plausible is that virtues (intellectual or otherwise) are character traits that one acquires and maintains through training and self-control. One is not born an impartial evaluator of evidence, for example, in the way that one might be born with good eyesight. Moreover, if one does not continue to be careful when assessing evidence, then over time one will lose this trait (good eyesight can be lost too, of course, but clearly it is not lost in the same way). In a sense, then, one's intellectual virtues offer a better insight into one's cognitive character than one's cognitive faculties, so if one wants one's virtue epistemology to capture the sense that when one gets things right it is down to one's cognitive character, then this might be a strike in favour of virtue responsibilism.

Relatedly, notice that intellectual virtues tend to be far more amenable to an epistemically internalist construal than cognitive faculties. We can, after all, imagine one's cognitive faculties functioning very reliably and yet one nonetheless possessing very little in the way of reflectively accessible grounds in support of the beliefs that one thereby forms (think of Chuck, our chicken-sexer). This is not so plausible when it comes to the intellectual virtues, and that is why epistemic internalists who are attracted to virtue epistemology tend to opt for virtue responsibilism.

Take the example of the conscientious and impartial evaluator of evidence, for example. What would it mean in this case for the agent to exhibit this intellectual virtue and yet lack good reflectively accessible grounds for any beliefs that she forms on this basis? In this sense, then, virtue responsibilists, like epistemic internalists more generally, think that when one has knowledge one also has a justification (internalistically construed) for one's belief in the target proposition.

Finally, recall that we noted above that a key part of all virtue epistemologies is the idea that an agent's cognitive traits need to be appropriately integrated within the agent's cognitive character if they are to lead that agent to knowledge. Those virtue epistemologists who are attracted to epistemic internalism will tend to interpret this demand in a more austere way than those attracted to epistemic externalism. In particular, virtue responsibilists will claim that such integration essentially involves gaining a *reflective* perspective on one's cognitive abilities, such that one does not simply employ them, but also has good reflectively accessible grounds to back up that employment (e.g., one has grounds for thinking that they are reliable, a reflective grip on why they are reliable, and so on). Virtue responsibilists think that such an austere reading of cognitive integration is required if we are to capture appropriately the sense of cognitive responsibility that is involved in acquiring knowledge.

There is thus a case that can be made for virtue responsibilism, though note that whether one is ultimately attracted to this view will largely depend on whether one is attracted to epistemic internalism about knowledge more generally. After all, those unpersuaded by the case for epistemic internalism will be unlikely to be persuaded by the considerations just noted in favour of virtue responsibilism that tends to trade on internalist intuitions that the epistemic externalist rejects. We will be revisiting the epistemic externalist/internalist distinction in chapter 5.

Modest virtue epistemology

Early virtue epistemic proposals tended to be quite modest in ambition. That is, they did not seek to offer a complete definition of knowledge – indeed many eschewed the analytic project of offering an analysis of knowledge altogether – but were instead merely claiming that a substantial necessary condition on knowledge was that the agent's true belief should be a product of her cognitive character. Call this view *modest virtue epistemology* (the parallels to the *modest anti-luck epistemology* that we saw in chapter 2 should be clear). The reason why virtue epistemic proposals tended to ally themselves to modest virtue epistemology is that it seems that the virtue-theoretic condition on knowledge – i.e., the condition that one's true belief should be the product of one's cognitive character – will be unable to eliminate all kinds of knowledge-undermining luck. Put another way, the thought is that the virtue-theoretic component of knowledge, while being able to accommodate the ability intuition, cannot also accommodate the anti-luck intuition.

For example, consider again the Roddy case given in chapter 1. Arguably, Roddy's true belief *is* the product of his cognitive character. He is, after all, using cognitive traits that would have ordinarily resulted in a true belief in this environment – remember that in this case it is just bad luck that Roddy happens to be looking at a sheep-shaped object (the big hairy dog) rather than a sheep. So unless we insist that reliable cognitive abilities can never generate a false belief (and intuitively we don't want to insist that), it is hard to see why one would deny that Roddy's belief is the product of his cognitive character. And yet it remains that this fails to ensure that his belief is not true as a matter of luck, and hence does not ensure that he has knowledge.

Moreover, even if one opted for a virtue responsibilist view that insisted that only epistemic virtues provide a route to knowledge, one would still face this problem. Consider, for example, the following case:

Judy
Judy is a judge who is presently presiding over an important criminal trial. She forms her belief that the defendant is guilty by conscientiously weighing up the evidence presented. Unbeknownst to Judy, however, the evidence against the defendant has been fabricated to ensure a conviction. Nevertheless, her belief is true in that the defendant is indeed guilty.

Judy's belief is uncontroversially the product of her intellectual virtues, and not merely a product of her reliable cognitive faculties. Clearly, however, Judy does not know that the defendant is guilty, even though her belief is virtuously formed and true. This is thus a Gettier-style case that undermines even virtue responsibilism, construed as offering a complete definition of knowledge in terms of epistemic virtue.

There is a reason why one can formulate Gettier-style cases against virtue-theoretic accounts of knowledge, and it's basically the same reason why process reliabilism and the classical account of knowledge are subject to such cases. This is that one can form one's belief via a reliable cognitive faculty or an intellectual virtue and yet that belief can be false (just as one can reliably form a false belief, or justifiably form a false belief). Given this fact about virtue epistemology, it follows that all one needs to do to formulate a Gettier-style case is take an example where the agent is forming her belief via a reliable cognitive faculty or an intellectual virtue in such a way that it would ordinarily have resulted in a false belief and then add some quirk in the environment such that the agent happens to form a true belief regardless. Hey presto, you have a true belief that meets the rubric laid down by virtue epistemology for knowledge (on either construal), but which is nonetheless only true as a matter of luck. Hence, you have formulated a Gettier-style counterexample to virtue epistemology.

Proponents of modest virtue epistemology thus argue that rather than offering a complete virtue-theoretic account of knowledge they are instead only offering, at best, an analysis of knowledge that covers a wide range of cases which don't involve Gettier-style epistemic luck. We can formulate this position as follows.

Modest Virtue Epistemology
S knows that *p* if and only if *S*'s true non-Gettierised belief that *p* is the product of the reliable cognitive abilities that make up her cognitive character.

Note that those attracted to virtue responsibilism will opt for a formulation of modest virtue epistemology that replaces cognitive abilities with intellectual virtues.

Robust virtue epistemology

By being less ambitious in what it sets out to do, modest virtue epistemology can side-step the problem posed by Gettier cases. Interestingly, some virtue epistemologists have argued that this pessimism about offering a virtue-theoretic response to Gettier-style cases is premature. Instead, they argue that all that is required is a more demanding formulation of the virtue-theoretic thesis. One can then offer a complete account of knowledge without having to appeal to any additional, non-virtue, epistemic conditions. Call this view *robust virtue epistemology* (the parallels to the *robust anti-luck epistemology* that we saw in chapter 2 should be clear).

Here is the sort of proposal that proponents of robust virtue epistemology opt for (construed as a form of virtue reliabilism rather than as a form of virtue responsibilism, though one can easily adapt it to suit if one wishes, by substituting intellectual virtues for cognitive abilities).

Robust Virtue Epistemology
S knows that *p* if and only if *S*'s belief that *p* is true because it was formed via the reliable cognitive abilities that make up her cognitive character.

On the face of it, this may not seem that different from the virtue reliabilist thesis described above, which we noted was unable to deal with Gettier-style cases. Notice, however, that the addition of the 'because' relation here has some important ramifications. In order to see this, let us consider a couple of cases.

First off, let's return to the Roddy case. Here we have a true belief that is virtuously formed, but which is not knowledge. Crucially, however, this belief is not true *because* of the operation of Roddy's cognitive character. Instead, and even despite the fact that intuitively this belief is in some sense the *product* of Roddy's cognitive character, it is the fact that there happens to be a sheep hidden from view behind the sheep-shaped object that ultimately ensures that his belief is true. That is, his belief is true *because* of the presence of the sheep in the field, and not because of the operation of Roddy's cognitive character. The same goes for other Gettier-style cases, such as the Smith and Jones case. Again, we here have a true belief that is virtuously formed but which is not knowledge. Notice, however, that the reason why Smith's belief is true has very little to do with his cognitive character, but is rather simply because of an incidental feature of the situation (that Smith happens to have ten coins in his pocket). In general, then, it seems that robust virtue epistemology can deal with knowledge-undermining epistemic luck without needing to incorporate an anti-luck condition.

There is some debate about how best to understand the 'because' relation in play here. The most natural way of reading this relation (we will consider a second reading in a moment) is that to say that the truth of an agent's belief is because of her cognitive character is to say that her cognitive character offers the *best causal explanation* of why her belief is true (i.e., that it is the most salient factor in a causal explanation of why the agent's belief is true). Consider again the Roddy case. When we say that the truth of Roddy's belief is not because of his cognitive character we are saying (according to this reading of 'because') that the most salient factor in a causal explanation of why Roddy's belief is true is not his cognitive character but rather something else (in this case, that there happens to be a sheep hidden from view behind the big hairy dog). On this reading, then, the mistake that modest virtue epistemology makes is to fail to see that it is not enough for the agent's true belief to be merely the *product* of her cognitive character, since that is compatible with the agent's cognitive character not being the most salient factor in a causal explanation of why the belief is true. In contrast, by inserting the 'because' relation into the account, robust virtue epistemology is able to avoid this pitfall, and in so doing can handle cases of knowledge-undermining epistemic luck that modest virtue epistemology is unable to deal with.

There is a further advantage to construing knowledge along the lines proposed by robust virtue epistemology. We can summarise this way of thinking about knowledge as the view that knowledge is cognitive success (i.e., true belief) that is because of cognitive ability. Interestingly, notice that one plausible rendering of the notion of an achievement is a success that is because of ability. If that's right, then it turns out that knowledge is just a kind of achievement, one that is specifically cognitive. That would be a nice result, since it would explain why knowledge is so important to us. Achievements, after all, are important to us, so it's unsurprising that we would also value specifically cognitive achievements – i.e., knowledge, on this view. (We will further explore the idea that achievements, and hence cognitive achievements, are of special value in chapter 7.)

Consider the notion that achievements are successes that are because of ability. There are three components here: the success, the ability, and the appropriate relationship (the 'because of') between them. Clearly an achievement requires success. An archer who is trying to hit a target with her bolt, but who misses, does not exhibit an achievement (at least not the achievement of hitting the target anyway). Moreover, skill is also required. A novice archer, with no ability, who hits the target with her bolt purely by luck does not exhibit an achievement. That just leaves the 'because of' element. Here it is important to note that one can 'Gettierize', and thereby undermine, achievements, just as one can with knowledge. Imagine an archer who skilfully fires her bolt at the target, and who hits the target, but where her success has nothing to do with her ability. Perhaps, for example, a dog catches the bolt mid-flight and deposits it in the target. I think it is evident that this isn't an achievement on the archer's part, even despite the presence of both skill and success. And the reason for this is that the success is not *because of* the skill on display, but is rather due to some other factor (e.g., the intervention of the dog).

With this account of achievements in play, however, it does look very much as if knowledge is simply a cognitive kind of achievement, and that clearly lends support to robust virtue epistemology.

Two problems for robust virtue epistemology

On the face of it, robust virtue epistemology offers an elegant, and fully adequate, account of knowledge. Unfortunately – or so I will argue at any rate – it doesn't work. I'm going to talk more about this in the next chapter, but there are two key counterexamples that demonstrate why I think the view is problematic.

The first is the Barney case that we considered in chapter 1. We noted there that although this case shares some features with standard Gettier-style cases, in that it is a case of a well-formed true belief that doesn't count as knowledge because of the luckiness of the true belief in question, it is not a normal Gettier-style case. The reason for this is that, unlike standard Gettier-style cases, the luck doesn't concern the relationship between the belief and the fact as such. For instance, compare this case with the Roddy case. Roddy doesn't actually get to see a sheep, even though his belief turns out to be true. Rather, something intervenes between his believing and the target fact, although his belief, by luck, is true anyway. Call this type of epistemic luck *intervening epistemic luck*. This is the usual kind of epistemic luck in play in most Gettier-style cases.

But not all. After all, Barney really does see a barn – there is no intervention here. The luckiness of the true belief so formed is thus purely to do with the fact that he is in an epistemically unfriendly environment, one in which he could very easily be led into making a cognitive error. That is, there is a very specific kind of knowledge-undermining epistemic luck in play here, what we will call *environmental epistemic luck*.

Robust virtue epistemology has a problem with such cases because, intuitively, Barney's cognitive ability *is* the most salient factor in a causal explanation of why his belief is true. After all, he really is looking at a genuine barn in cognitive conditions that are entirely appropriate for making an observation of this sort (e.g., the light is good, he is close enough to the barn, his eyesight is good, and so on). Why, then, would Barney's cognitive ability not be the most salient factor in a causal explanation of why his belief is true? It would thus appear that Barney should count as having knowledge by the lights of robust virtue epistemology, and yet there is a strong intuition that he does not have knowledge in this case due to the environmental epistemic luck in play.

Interestingly, this point applies to achievements more generally, and so undermines the idea that knowledge should be understood as a cognitive kind of achievement. We noted above that one can 'Gettierize', and thereby undermine, an achievement. The case we gave to illustrate this point, however – which involved a dog catching an arrow mid-flight and depositing it in the target – was clearly of the intervening sort. Imagine now a version of this case where the luck was purely environmental. Suppose our archer skilfully fires her bolt at the target, and successfully hits the target, without anything getting in the way. But imagine that there was, unbeknownst to our hero, a wind machine set up near the target designed to repel anything that is fired at it. Ordinarily, this wind machine would have been working, and so our hero would not have hit the target, but by a fluke the wind machine failed to work properly at the exact moment that our hero fired her bolt. It is thus a matter of luck that she succeeded, in that she could very easily have failed to hit the target. Put another way, there are lots of close possible worlds where she fails to hit the target because the wind machine repels the bolt. Even so, given that nothing intervened in this case, is it any less of an achievement on her part? Indeed, wouldn't we want to say that her success is, in this case, *because of* her archery abilities? If that's right, then achievements are compatible with environmental epistemic luck just as cognitive achievements seem to be (as the Barney case illustrates). Knowledge, however, isn't compatible with Gettier-style luck, whether of an intervening or an environmental variety, and hence the analogy between knowledge and (cognitive) achievements that the proponent of robust virtue epistemology wants to exploit breaks down.

Note, too, that that this problem is even worse if one considers a second reading of the 'because' relation that has been offered in the literature by defenders of robust virtue epistemology. On this reading, we are to think of the relation not in causal explanatory terms but rather in terms of a causal power, like fragility. When we say, for example, that the ornament broke because it was fragile the 'because' in play is not to be read (not normally anyway) as the 'because' of causal explanation. After all, this statement could be true and yet it not be the case that the most salient factor in a causal explanation of why the ornament broke is its fragility (the most salient factor could be that someone hit it with a hammer, or that the fixings holding it in place gave way). Instead, what we mean when we make a statement like this is just that the object in question had a causal power – i.e., roughly, a disposition to behave in a certain way in certain conditions – and it manifested that power. In this case, for example, what we mean is that the ornament was fragile and was manifesting this fragility when it broke. In the same way, one might argue that how we should read the 'because' relation in the formulation of robust virtue epistemology is along analogous lines such that the true belief in question merely needs to be appropriately manifesting the relevant cognitive dispositions of the agent which make up the agent's cognitive character.

One reason why one might be attracted to such an alternative reading of the 'because' relation is that causal explanations are normally thought of as highly context-sensitive. What may count as a good causal explanation of an event in one context might not count as a good explanation relative to a different context. As a result, by allying robust virtue epistemology to a causal explanatory account of the 'because' relation one may thereby import such context-sensitivity into one's view, a consequence that many epistemologists would not be happy with. What is important for our current purposes, however, is that opting for the causal power reading of the 'because' relation does not help one to respond to the problem posed by the Barney case. After all, it is even more plausible to suppose that Barney's true belief is appropriately manifesting the relevant cognitive dispositions that make up his cognitive character than that his cognitive character is the most salient factor in a causal explanation of the truth of his belief. Remember, Barney really does see the barn in cognitive conditions that are entirely appropriate for forming judgments of this sort.

There may be things that the proponent of a robust virtue epistemology (of either stripe) could say in response to the Barney case. She might argue, for example, that Barney does have knowledge in this case after all, despite first appearances. Or (if she opts for the causal explanatory reading of robust virtue epistemology anyway) she might argue that the most salient factor in the causal explanation of why Barney has a true belief is not his cognitive character, again despite first appearances. The former route does not look particularly appealing, since it involves in effect denying (or at least radically restricting) the anti-luck intuition. The latter option might look superficially more attractive, since one might think that cognitive abilities, like abilities more generally, are relative to suitable environments, and yet Barney, since he is in barn façade county, is not in a suitable environment for the exercise of the relevant cognitive abilities. Accordingly, it would follow that the most salient factor in the causal explanation of Barney's true belief is not his cognitive character after all, since in the relevant sense he is not exhibiting the target cognitive abilities. This response to the problem is not going to work, however, and it is worthwhile spending a few moments understanding why.

First off, note that all should agree that abilities, and thus cognitive abilities, should be understood relative to suitable environments. We would not evaluate your professed ability to play the piano, for example, by asking you to exhibit this ability underwater, since this is clearly not a suitable environment for the manifestation of this ability. Even so, notice that we do not individuate the relevant environment for an ability in a very fine-grained way, at least not unless the ability is very specifically defined (e.g., the ability to play the piano under water). When one plays piano outside, in a slightly cold mild breeze, for example, one is exhibiting the very same ability that one exhibits when one, say, plays the piano in a stuffy drawing room. Similarly, the cognitive abilities that Barney employs in this case are just the normal cognitive abilities that he would employ in a wide range of cases that involve identifying medium-sized objects at relatively close range in good cognitive conditions. That is, we would not naturally suppose that a special range of cognitive abilities is required in this environment, and hence there is no straightforward way of extracting from the observation that abilities should be understood relative to suitable environments the conclusion that Barney lacks the target cognitive abilities.

Still, the proponent of this virtue-theoretic response to the Barney case might argue that, contrary to intuition, we should opt for a more fine-grained account of the way in which cognitive abilities are relative to suitable environments. Even if they did take this route, however, it is still not clear that it would offer them a way out of the problem. After all, notice that it is in fact incidental to the Barney case that there are actually barn façades in his environment, for all that is required to make his belief only luckily true is that he could so very easily have been mistaken, and we can ensure that by simply setting up the case so that there are barn façades present in near-by possible worlds. With the case so described, however, then the problem in play here will remain no matter how finely grained one individuates abilities relative to suitable environments.

In order to see this, think again about the ability to play the piano. Suppose that one is playing the piano in normal piano-playing conditions but that, unbeknownst to one, in a wide class of near-by possible worlds the room that one is playing in is full of water. Now ask yourself which ability one is manifesting in this case. Is it one's normal piano-playing ability, or is it a special ability to play the piano relative to an environment in which one could so very easily have been underwater? I think it is clear that it is the former, and what this case demonstrates is that it can be a matter of luck that one is in suitable conditions to manifest an ability. If one transplants this point back to the cognitive realm, however, then it undermines the envisaged virtue-theoretic response to the Barney case. For when the Barney case is described such that the barn façades are only in the near-by possible worlds and not in the actual world, then the case becomes analogous in the relevant respects to the piano example just given. Accordingly, we should draw the same moral: that the cognitive abilities being exhibited here are normal cognitive abilities, and thus that Barney is not attempting, and failing, to exhibit a special cognitive ability which is relative to an unusual environment. Rather, he is simply exhibiting his normal cognitive abilities and thereby gaining a true belief, albeit one that could very easily have been false.

The Barney case thus poses a pretty tough problem for robust virtue epistemology. Moreover, once this type of case is put together with a second counterexample, the view starts to look to be in serious trouble. While the Barney case seems to show that the robust virtue epistemological view is not demanding enough – in that it credits agents with knowledge that, intuitively, they do not have – the second type of counterexample appears to show that the view is *too* demanding – i.e., it fails to credit agents with knowledge that, intuitively, they possess. The best example to illustrate this point is that of testimonial knowledge which involves a significant degree of trust. Consider the following example.

Jenny
Jenny gets off the train in an unfamiliar city and asks the first person that she meets for directions. The person that she asks is indeed knowledgeable about the area, and helpfully gives her directions. Jenny believes what she is told and goes on her way to her intended destination.

Now, unless we have an awful lot less knowledge than we usually suppose, it ought to be possible for Jenny to gain knowledge in this way. Notice that in crediting Jenny with knowledge in this case we are assuming that she is at least sensitive to possible problems with trusting the first person she meets. For example, we would expect her to spot an obvious lie were she to be told one, and we are taking it for granted that she wouldn't ask someone who would in all likelihood manifestly be unreliable (such as a small child). Gullibility is not a route to (testimonial) knowledge. Moreover, I take it that we are also assuming that this is an epistemically friendly environment in the relevant respects (e.g., that the inhabitants of this city aren't all compulsive liars), and also that there is nothing that Jenny ought to be aware of which would indicate (falsely) that it is an epistemically unfriendly environment (e.g., a big public information sign that says not to trust testimony from the locals). The point of the example is that Jenny does not make any special checks to ensure that she can trust this informant. Nevertheless, that doesn't seem necessary; it seems that she can gain knowledge in this way even without making such special checks, at least *modulo* all the *caveats* just made (i.e., that we wouldn't just believe anything she is told, and so on). Put another way, the moral of the example seems to be that trust in an informant can play a significant role in the acquisition of testimonial knowledge.

The problem for proponents of robust virtue epistemology, however, is that while it does seem that Jenny has knowledge in this case, and while she has manifested some cognitive ability (e.g., in that she wouldn't believe anything she is told), it doesn't appear right to say that the most salient factor in the causal explanation for why she has a true belief is her cognitive ability. Indeed, if anything, the most salient factor in this causal explanation seems to be the cognitive ability of her informant. There is thus a *prima facie* case for supposing that the proponents of robust virtue epistemology must deny that Jenny has knowledge, but this is counterintuitive.

As before, there are moves that the robust virtue epistemologist might make in response to this case. For example, she might bite the bullet and argue that Jenny doesn't have knowledge after all, despite first appearances. The problem with taking this route, of course, is that it puts a great deal of our testimonial knowledge under threat, since don't we gain a great deal of this kind of knowledge by, for the most part, trusting others? Alternatively, the robust virtue epistemologist might try to argue that Jenny's cognitive ability *is* the most salient factor in the causal explanation of why she has a true belief, again despite first appearances. But then that seems incompatible with the apparently undeniable fact that a great deal of trust with regard to Jenny's informant is involved.

Whatever the robust virtue epistemologist argues, however, it is clear that such cases put the view under pressure, and when such cases are combined with the Barney case just discussed, the proposal starts to look to be on very shaky ground indeed. The point is that while the Barney case calls for a *strengthening* of robust virtue epistemology, the Jenny case calls for a *weakening* of robust virtue epistemology. Thus, whatever moves one makes to resolve the one problem make it harder to resolve the other problem, with the result being that robust virtue epistemology is torn asunder.

The upshot of the failure of robust virtue epistemology is that while virtue-theoretic proposals are very good at accommodating the ability intuition, they are quite poor at accommodating other core cases of knowledge. In particular, robust virtue epistemology is unable to fully accommodate the anti-luck intuition, since it allows cases of lucky true belief (like the Barney case) to count as knowledge. Thus one cannot fully accommodate the anti-luck intuition by appealing to robust virtue epistemology, even though this proposal is very good at accounting for the ability intuition. Moreover, robust virtue epistemology also cannot accommodate cases in which one gains one's knowledge by, to a significant degree, trusting others, as demonstrated by the Jenny case. Robust virtue epistemology is thus both too demanding and simultaneously not demanding enough, as a theory of knowledge.

Concluding remarks

So where does all this leave us? Well, it seems we are back to modest virtue epistemology, in that virtue epistemology is unable to offer us a complete account of knowledge. In particular, it appears that virtue epistemology is unable to offer us an account of knowledge that can deal with all kinds of knowledge-undermining luck. As we will see in the next chapter, one way of responding to this weakness on the part of virtue epistemology is to re-examine the core intuitions about knowledge that we are trying to respond to in offering a theory of this notion.

Chapter summary

We saw that one way of motivating *virtue epistemology* – or at least one version of virtue epistemology anyway, known as *virtue reliabilism* – was as viewing it as a more refined version of *process reliabilism*. Whereas the latter allows any reliable belief-forming process to generate knowledge, virtue reliabilism instead insists that only those reliable belief-forming processes that make up one's cognitive character – such as one's cognitive faculties, cognitive abilities, and intellectual virtues – can generate knowledge. This refinement allows virtue reliabilism to deal with certain cases that process reliabilism struggles with, such as cases where the reliability on display has nothing to do with the subject's manifestation of cognitive ability (e.g., the Temp case) and cases involving cognitive malfunction (e.g., the Alvin case). Virtue reliabilism can be contrasted with *virtue responsibilism*, where the latter holds that the exercise of intellectual virtue is essential to the acquisition of knowledge (i.e., such that the mere exercise of cognitive faculties or abilities will not suffice). A distinction was drawn between *modest virtue epistemology* and *robust virtue epistemology*. While the former allows there to be other epistemic conditions on knowledge over and above the virtue condition, the latter attempts to exclusively analyse knowledge in terms of a virtue condition. Part of the rationale for modest virtue epistemology is that it can seem that no virtue condition on its own – whether cast along virtue reliabilist or virtue responsibilist lines – can exclude Gettier-style cases. Robust virtue epistemology, however, attempts to deal with Gettier-style cases by insisting that knowledge is true belief that is *because* of the exercise of cognitive ability (or intellectual virtue, if one is a virtue responsibilist). This deals with most Gettier-style cases because while they involve a true belief and the exercise of cognitive ability, it is often the case that the true belief is not because of the exercise of cognitive ability. A further advantage to this proposal is that it seems to make knowledge a particularly cognitive kind of achievement, in that achievements more generally seem to be successes that are because of ability. Robust virtue epistemology faces some problems, however. First, with a distinction between *intervening epistemic luck* and *environmental epistemic luck* in play, we can show that there seem to be some Gettier-style cases, such as the Barney case, which satisfy the rubric laid down by robust virtue epistemology, and hence ought to be counted as knowledge. Second, robust virtue epistemology struggles to account for the kind of testimonial knowledge one can gain by, for the most part, trusting a reliable informant. These two objections are collectively quite tricky for robust virtue epistemology in that while the first objection effectively maintains that the view is not demanding enough, the second objection effectively maintains that the view is too demanding. It is thus hard to simultaneously offer a solution to both problems.

Further introductory reading

For a very introductory overview of virtue epistemology, see Pritchard (2013, ch. 6). For some other useful overviews of virtue epistemology, see Battaly (2008) and Kvanvig (2011). For an excellent annotated bibliography of recent work on virtue epistemology, see Turri & Sosa (2010).

Further advanced reading

See Goldman (1986) for the key statement of (a version of) process reliabilism. Sosa (1991) is the seminal work for discussions of virtue epistemology. See Greco (1999; 2000) for a defence of virtue reliabilism. See also Plantinga (1993) for a related view, and for the original statement of the Alvin case (p. 199). For some of the main defences of robust virtue epistemology, see Zagzebski (1996; 1999), Sosa (2007; 2009; 2011; 2015), and Greco (2009a). For a key defence of virtue responsibilism, see Zagzebski (1996). For an excellent account of the distinction between virtue reliabilism and virtue responsibilism, see Axtell (1997). For an influential discussion of virtue epistemology, see Kvanvig (1992). The Jenny case is modelled on a case offered by Lackey (2007), though beware that Lackey's case is slightly different (which is why the protagonist is named 'Jenny' and not 'Jennifer'), and is directed at making a much stronger point (roughly, though Lackey doesn't quite put it in these terms, that one can gain testimonial knowledge without exhibiting any cognitive agency at all). The distinction between intervening and environmental epistemic luck, and the point that this works against robust virtue epistemology, is due to Pritchard – see especially Pritchard (2009b; 2012a) and Pritchard, Millar & Haddock (2010, chapters 2–4). For a recent development of this idea, see Kallestrup & Pritchard (2014).

Free internet resources

See Greco & Turri (2011) for an excellent overview of recent work on virtue epistemology. See also Baehr (2004).

Study questions

1. Explain what process reliabilism is, and describe at least two problems that it is held to face.
2. What is virtue reliabilism, and how does it differ from process reliabilism?
3. What is the difference between, on the one hand, a cognitive faculty or ability and, on the other hand, an intellectual virtue?
4. What is the difference between virtue reliabilism and virtue responsibilism? Try to explain in your own words why this distinction tends to line-up behind the epistemic externalism/internalism distinction regarding knowledge.
5. Try to explain, in your own words, how the virtue reliabilist attempts to capture the idea that knowledge requires taking cognitive responsibility for one's beliefs without thereby endorsing epistemic internalism.

6 Why might one think that the Gettier problem is as much a problem for virtue responsibilism as it is for virtue reliabilism?
7 What is modest virtue epistemology, and how does it differ from robust virtue epistemology?
8 Why might one think that knowledge is a kind of achievement? Is it?
9 How does robust virtue epistemology try to deal with Gettier-style cases?
10 What is the distinction between intervening and environmental epistemic luck, and how does it bear on the plausibility of robust virtue epistemology?
11 Why might testimonial knowledge that is largely gained through trust pose a problem for robust virtue epistemology?

Sample essay questions
1 What is virtue reliabilism, and what advantages does it have, if any, over process reliabilism?
2 Critically compare and contrast virtue reliabilism and virtue responsibilism. Which is more persuasive, do you think?
3 How does robust virtue epistemology attempt to resolve the Gettier problem? Is it successful?
4 Should knowledge be understood as a kind of achievement? Explain what this proposal involves, and critically evaluate its prospects.

4
Anti-Luck Virtue Epistemology

Recap

We noted back in chapter 1, when we were considering the question of how to analyse knowledge, that there are two overarching intuitions about knowledge. The first – the *ability intuition* – was that knowledge is due to cognitive ability. The second – the *anti-luck intuition* – was that knowledge excludes luck. When we first introduced these two intuitions about knowledge we also noted that one could regard them as closely related. What does it take to ensure that one's true belief is not due to luck? Well, that it is the product of one's cognitive ability. Conversely, insofar as one's true belief is the product of one's cognitive ability, then one would expect it to thereby be immune to knowledge-undermining luck.

Even so, as we have discussed in the last two chapters, one could regard one of these intuitions as the dominant intuition, with the other intuition in some sense subservient. In chapter 2, we looked at a robust anti-luck epistemology that in effect treats the anti-luck intuition as dominant. On this view, knowledge is essentially non-lucky true belief. Hence, this proposal holds that the reason why we have the ability intuition is because we have the anti-luck intuition (i.e., we care about gaining true beliefs through one's cognitive ability because we care about avoiding knowledge-undermining luck). Unfortunately, we also saw that this proposal was unsatisfactory. On the best account available of how the anti-luck condition might be formulated, which we saw involved appeal to the safety principle, there were still problems remaining. In particular, there are cases in which agents meet this anti-luck condition and yet do not know. Moreover, our intuition about why they lack knowledge in such cases is clearly that the true beliefs so formed are not the product of the agent's cognitive ability (as in the Temp case, where the subject's safe true beliefs have nothing significantly to do with his manifestation of cognitive ability). In short, a robust anti-luck epistemology cannot accommodate the ability intuition.

In chapter 3 we then turned to robust virtue epistemology, a proposal that in effect treats the ability intuition as the dominant intuition. On this view, knowledge is in essence true belief that is the product of cognitive ability. Hence, this proposal holds that the reason why we have the anti-luck intuition is because we have the ability intuition (i.e., we care about gaining true beliefs that are immune to knowledge-undermining luck because we care about gaining true beliefs by cognitive ability). Unfortunately, we saw that this approach didn't work either. On the one hand, there are cases in which agents have knowledge and yet they don't meet the rather demanding virtue-theoretic account of knowledge that is laid down in order to deal with knowledge-undermining epistemic luck (e.g., the Jenny case, involving testimonial knowledge largely gained via trust). On the other hand, there are cases in which agents meet the relevant virtue-theoretic condition and yet lack knowledge because of the presence of knowledge-undermining epistemic luck (e.g., the Barney case, which specifically involves environmental, rather than intervening, epistemic luck). This second kind of case is more significant for our purposes, since it shows that a robust virtue epistemology cannot accommodate the anti-luck intuition.

Thus, neither a robust anti-luck epistemology nor a robust virtue epistemology gives us what we are looking for, since neither view can simultaneously account for both of these core intuitions about knowledge.

Anti-luck virtue epistemology

We are thus back with the two intuitions that we began with without an account on the table that is able to treat either intuition appropriately as dominant. This should make us pause to reconsider how these two intuitions are related. I want to suggest that the proper way to think about the relationship between these two intuitions is that they pose two distinct demands on knowledge (which, as we will see, is not to say that they impose *independent* demands on knowledge).

On reflection, this should be just as we expect. If luck is a modal notion in roughly the way described in chapter 2, then an anti-luck condition will inevitably involve a modal epistemic principle like safety or sensitivity. But if that's right, then it is unsurprising that one could satisfy such a condition while not exhibiting any cognitive ability, since whatever modal requirement is imposed, with enough imagination one could think of a way in which it can be satisfied in a manner that bears no relation to the agent's cognitive abilities. After all, any such modal condition will merely specify that one's beliefs and the facts match across an appropriate range of worlds. But such a matching might have nothing at all to do with one's own cognitive agency, but could be due to entirely independent factors, as the Temp case illustrates.

Similarly, on reflection there is no reason why forming a true belief through cognitive ability should suffice to meet the relevant anti-luck condition. Indeed, wasn't that one of the morals of Gettier-style cases? More generally, as we saw in chapter 3, one's manifestation of ability (cognitive or otherwise), even when that manifestation suffices to generate an achievement on our part (at least as far as robust virtue epistemologists understand this notion anyway), can nonetheless be *fragile*, in the sense that the success in question could have easily been a failure. That's why the Barney case, which we saw can count as a cognitive achievement in the relevant sense, is also a case in which the target belief does not amount to knowledge on account of the knowledge-undermining epistemic luck in play.

In the absence of a theoretical motivation to opt for either a robust virtue epistemology or a robust anti-luck epistemology, one might naturally opt for a view that combines both conditions, what we can call an *anti-luck virtue epistemology*. We need to tread carefully here, however, since merely combining an anti-luck condition (i.e., safety) with a virtue condition won't work, as it will be subject to straightforward counterexamples. Consider, for example, this crude formulation of anti-luck virtue epistemology:

Anti-Luck Virtue Epistemology: First Pass
S knows that p if and only if (i) S's true belief that p is safe, and (ii) it was formed via the reliable cognitive abilities that make up S's cognitive character.

(Note that if one is attracted to virtue responsibilism, then one should consider replacing 'cognitive abilities' in this formulation with 'intellectual virtues'. I will be setting this complication to one side in what follows.)

It is easy to create counterexamples to this formulation. All one needs to do is set things up such that the reasons why the subject's belief is safe have nothing to do with her manifestation of cognitive ability. Indeed, we don't even need a new example, as Temp will suffice. Temp's belief is obviously safe, since given how he is forming his beliefs he is guaranteed to be right. Condition (i) is thus met. But so is condition (ii). Temp, after all, is doing just the right thing that one should do if one wants to find out what the temperature in the room is, which is to look at a thermometer. Remember that he has no reason to think that the thermometer is broken or that conditions are not normal. There is thus a perfectly reasonable sense in which Temp's beliefs about the temperature in the room were the product of his reliable cognitive abilities. And yet Temp doesn't know what the temperature in the room is.

That Temp satisfies the conditions laid down by our crude formulation of anti-luck virtue epistemology should remind us what is really at issue in this case. The reason why Temp lacks knowledge is that although he is exercising his cognitive abilities, and although his true beliefs so formed are safe, the latter has very little to do with the former. In particular, what is explaining why his beliefs are safe has almost nothing to do with his exercise of cognitive ability and almost everything to do with the activities of the hidden helper. What we are looking for in an anti-luck virtue epistemology is thus not a proposal which treats the anti-luck condition and the ability/virtue condition as completely independent, but rather one which demands an explanatory relationship between the subject's safe cognitive success and their exercise of cognitive ability.

This is the kind of formulation that we need (where for ease of expression we are using the phrase 'cognitive success' instead of 'true belief'):

Anti-Luck Virtue Epistemology
S knows that *p* if, and only if, S's safe cognitive success is the manifestation of S's relevant cognitive abilities, where this safe cognitive success is to a significant degree creditable to S's manifestation of those cognitive abilities.

Notice the key difference between this formulation and the last one, in that rather than treating the anti-luck and ability/virtue conditions as completely independent, we are instead demanding that there be an explanatory relation between them. Note too the kind of explanatory relation in play, which is both in a sense weaker, and in another sense stronger, than that at issue with regard to robust virtue epistemology. Recall that robust virtue epistemology demanded that the cognitive success had to be *because of* the subject's manifestation of cognitive ability, where this meant that the subject's manifestation of cognitive ability had to be the overarching element in a causal explanation of her cognitive success. Robust virtue epistemology needed the explanatory relation to be this strong in order to deal with Gettier-style cases though, as we saw, in the end even by having such a strong explanatory relation in play it still couldn't deal with all of such cases (in particular, it couldn't deal with the Barney case). We don't require our explanatory relation to be so strong since we can deal with Gettier-style cases by incorporating the safety condition. What we do need, however, is the idea that the subject's safe cognitive success is at least *significantly creditable* to the subject's manifestation of her cognitive abilities, where this means that her manifestation of her cognitive abilities must play some significant role in the causal explanation of her cognitive success (we will consider an example in a moment).

This brings us to the sense in which the explanatory relation at issue in this formulation of anti-luck virtue epistemology is stronger than that at issue in robust virtue epistemology. According to robust virtue epistemology, what mattered was only that the subject's cognitive success stand in the appropriate explanatory relation to her cognitive ability. But what anti-luck virtue epistemology demands is that the subject's *safe cognitive success* needs to stand in the appropriate explanatory relation to her cognitive ability. We can see why this is important by returning to the Temp case. For what goes wrong in the Temp case is not that his cognitive abilities fail to play any significant role in him forming a true belief, but rather that they play no significant role in explaining why his true belief is safe, with this instead being explained by the intervention of the hidden helper.

Now that we have a clear idea of what anti-luck virtue epistemology demands, we can ask whether it can handle all the usual problem cases. The Gettier-style cases, including non-standard Gettier-style cases, like the Barney case, are dealt with by the anti-luck condition, since in all of these cases we have a true belief that is unsafe. The same goes for other kinds of cases relative to which the safety condition fares well, such as the Lottie case and the Ernie case, which were considered in chapter 2. In short, this account will have all the advantages of an anti-luck epistemology.

Moreover, the kind of cases that robust anti-luck epistemology cannot deal with are dealt with by demanding that the subject's safe cognitive success should be significantly creditable her cognitive ability. We have just seen how this works with the Temp case, and the reasoning that applied there will also deal with the Mathemi case that we encountered in chapter 2, and which has the same general structure. Consider also the Alvin case from chapter 3, where the subject was forming her true belief via a cognitive malfunction, albeit a reliable one. Since the belief-forming process in play is reliable, we can expect it to issue in safe true beliefs. Clearly, however, the safety of such beliefs so formed will not be significantly creditable to the subject's cognitive ability. Instead, it is in spite of her cognitive abilities that these beliefs are safely true.

Moreover, notice that since we have not 'beefed up' the ability condition in terms of adding a 'because' clause in the manner of robust virtue epistemology, we do not need to worry about cases like the Jenny case. Remember that we made clear in our discussion of the case that Jenny is displaying a significant degree of cognitive ability in forming her belief, such that her safe cognitive success is to a significant degree creditable to her cognitive agency (e.g., she doesn't just ask anyone; she would be sensitive to relevant defeaters were they to be present, and so on). The key point here is that an agent can form a safe true belief through cognitive ability in the relevant sense without it being the case that her cognitive ability is the most salient feature in a causal explanation of that safe cognitive success. Instead, all that is required is that the agent's cognitive ability plays a significant role in the causal explanation of that safe cognitive success. Jenny's belief can thus meet the lower standard demanded by anti-luck virtue epistemology.

We thus seem to have an entirely adequate theory of knowledge, in that it can account for our most fundamental intuitions about what it is to have knowledge. Are we, *qua* epistemologists, home and dry?

The nature of anti-luck virtue epistemology

What kind of a theory of knowledge is anti-luck virtue epistemology? One point to note in this regard is that it is essentially a *structural* proposal, in that it leaves open a number of different permutations. For example, just as with robust virtue epistemology, we can imagine both epistemically externalist and epistemically internalist renderings of this theory. In the version offered above, the focus is on cognitive abilities, which almost certainly tends towards an epistemically externalist rendering of the view, in that standardly one can manifest such abilities without being in possession of any supporting reflectively accessible rational support for one's belief (i.e., while lacking a justification for one's belief, classically conceived). Think, for example, of the kind of virtue reliabilism that we encountered in the last chapter. But no harm would be done to the account if we insisted that the relevant notion of cognitive agency in play should be the intellectual virtues specifically. One would thus have a version of anti-luck virtue epistemology that was more in the spirit of virtue responsibilism rather than virtue reliabilism.

A related question we might ask is whether anti-luck virtue epistemology is a *reductive* theory of knowledge. Recall that in chapter 1 we noted that the philosophical project we are concerned with here, in common with mainstream epistemology more generally, is the analytical project of offering necessary and sufficient conditions for knowledge, where this is construed in a fairly modest fashion (you may find it useful to remind yourself of what we said on this score). We noted that, ideally at least, an analysis should be reductive, in the sense that it analyses knowledge in terms that do not themselves make use of the term 'knowledge'. A failure to offer a reductive account does not mean that the analytical project is hopeless, however, since even an analysis that is ultimately circular can be informative (we will consider an example in a moment). Still, there is clearly something lacking in a circular analysis of knowledge.

So far we have been assuming that the various analyses of knowledge that we have been considering, such as robust anti-luck epistemology or robust virtue epistemology, are reductive analyses. They certainly seem to be reductive analyses, since they don't make any *explicit* mention of knowledge in the analysis. Nonetheless, whether an analysis of knowledge is really reductive depends very much on the detail of the view. With that in mind, we might now legitimately ask whether anti-luck virtue epistemology offers us a reductive analysis of knowledge.

The big question in this regard – and this is an issue that bears on all virtue-theoretic accounts of knowledge – is whether one can specify cognitive abilities in knowledge-independent terms. On the face of it one might think so, since it seems we can identify them in terms of their reliability and their integration within the agent's cognitive character as a whole. The worry, however, is whether, ultimately, whatever detailed account we give of cognitive ability will end up saying that they are the kinds of belief-forming traits that are knowledge-conducive. If that were the case, then clearly a reductive account of knowledge would be out of the question. (Interestingly, although the reasons are more complicated, a related concern might also apply to our understanding of the safety condition, though this is a point that often overlooked by epistemologists.)

It would take us too far from our present concerns to explore this issue further here. One point that is worth making, however, is that even if anti-luck virtue epistemology is unable to offer a reductive account of knowledge, it would still constitute an informative analysis. After all, it is clearly philosophical progress to discover that knowledge has this two-part structure. Thus, the analytical project does not stand or fall in terms of its ability to offer a reductive analysis of knowledge.

Diagnosis

One question that we might ask about anti-luck virtue epistemology is why knowledge has this two-aspect structure in the first place, in that it is responsive both to the avoidance of luck and to the manifestation of cognitive ability. Indeed, one might maintain that at least robust virtue epistemology and robust anti-luck epistemology have the advantage of being wonderfully simple theories of knowledge.

One way of motivating anti-luck virtue epistemology in this regard is by arguing that it demonstrates the *epistemic dependence* of knowledge. By this I mean the extent to which whether one's true belief amounts to knowledge can be significantly dependent upon factors external to one's cognitive agency. Notice that the two types of problem case that we posed for robust virtue epistemology effectively demonstrate that there is both a positive and a negative dimension to epistemic dependence. *Negative epistemic dependence* is when one exhibits a very high level of cognitive ability – a level that would normally be comfortably sufficient for knowledge – and yet one fails to know because of factors external to one's cognitive agency. The Barney case is an instance of this, where it is the environmental epistemic luck that prevents the subject from having knowledge. *Positive epistemic dependence* is when one exhibits a relatively low level of cognitive ability – i.e., lower than one normally exhibits when one acquires knowledge – and yet one gains knowledge nonetheless because of factors external to one's cognitive agency. The Jenny case is an instance of this, in that although she manifests relatively little cognitive ability, given the kind of environment she is in, and in particular the reliability of her informant, she nonetheless comes to have knowledge.

Once one grants that there is this interplay between factors internal and external to one's cognitive agency when one has knowledge, then one would expect knowledge to have the kind of two-aspect structure as set-out by anti-luck virtue epistemology. In particular, one would expect that sometimes – in particular, when conditions are particularly epistemically favourable, and so having a safe cognitive success is relatively straightforward – a relatively low level of cognitive ability can suffice for knowledge. This is why one can often gain testimonial knowledge largely (though not completely) through trust, as Jenny does. In contrast, when conditions are epistemically unfavourable, such as when one's belief would be subject to high levels of epistemic luck, then manifesting the usual level of cognitive ability will not be enough. This is why Barney lacks knowledge, despite the cognitive abilities that he displays.

A second way of confronting this issue about what motivates anti-luck virtue epistemology is by undertaking a thought-experiment that has been suggested as a way of casting light on the nature of knowledge. Picture an imaginary society that lacked the concept of knowledge. Why might the inhabitants of this society feel the need to introduce it? Well, notice first that it would be very practically useful to have some way of picking out good informants – i.e., informants who can help us to find out the truth on matters that interest us. We could thus imagine a concept very like knowledge – a kind of proto-knowledge concept – being employed for just this purpose. Call this proto-knowledge, knowledge*, and anyone who possesses knowledge* a knower*. The idea is then that it would be useful to label good informants as knowers*, and accordingly to label the accurate information that they offer on subjects about which they are good informants, knowledge*.

So, for example, imagine that John lives on a hill and so has a particularly good view of what is happening in the valley below (and he is generally truthful and helpful, etc.). He would thus be a good informant when it comes to a range of propositions concerning what is happening in the valley. It would clearly be practically useful to us to flag the fact that John is a good informant in this regard, and we can do this by calling him a knower* as regards these propositions, in that his true beliefs in these propositions amount to knowledge*.

Note that knowledge* is not yet like our concept of knowledge. For one thing, the concept only applies to other people's true beliefs, while we also use the concept of knowledge to classify our own beliefs. In addition, in deciding whether an agent is a knower* we are only assessing how good an informant he is relative to the actual circumstances that he finds himself in – i.e., the 'live' error-possibilities that are in play in their environment. In the case of John just described, for example, all that is at issue is whether he has a good view of the valley and the ability (and inclination) to make use of this advantage. The salient error-possibilities when it comes to the question of whether he has knowledge* are thus things like whether there is something in his environment which is obscuring his view (a heavy fog, say). Note, however, that our concept of knowledge treats a far greater range of error-possibilities as salient. In particular, it is also responsive to potential error-possibilities, even if they are not actual. (Recall the anti-luck intuition, one consequence of which is that the fact that you could very easily have been deceived is a ground to deny you knowledge, even if in fact you were not deceived.)

Interestingly, however, we would expect the proto-concept that is designed to pick out good informants to evolve over time so that it begins to resemble our concept of knowledge. For example, we could imagine knowledge* ultimately being used to classify oneself and not just others, and the application of the concept being 'stretched' so that it is responsive to non-actual but potential error-possibilities, and not just the actual ones. Over time, then, knowledge* might evolve into knowledge.

Many philosophers find this so-called *genealogical* account of the source of the concept of knowledge to be very persuasive. In particular, virtue epistemologists often cite this story as offering support for their view. After all, this account of the source of the concept of knowledge puts good informants at the heart of the story, and one natural way of thinking about what constitutes a good informant is that she is an informant who is exercising a reliable cognitive ability (think, for example, of the case of John just described). This would thus appear to suggest that what is most central to the concept of knowledge is the ability intuition, which is the primary concern of virtue epistemology. Interestingly, however, once we start to think about this account of the source of the concept of knowledge in more detail, it becomes apparent that it actually lends greater support to anti-luck virtue epistemology than it does to virtue epistemology.

In particular, while there is clearly something right about the suggestion that a good informant is a reliable informant, this does not play into the hands of the virtue epistemologist in the manner that it may at first appear. The reason for this is that there is an important ambiguity in the very notion of a reliable (and hence good) informant. In one sense, it means an informant who possesses a reliable cognitive ability with regard to the target subject matter (and who is willing to sincerely communicate what she believes, something that we will take for granted in what follows). In another sense, it means an informant whom one can rely on (i.e., whose information will not lead you astray).

Now one might naturally think that this is a distinction without a difference, in that informants who possess reliable cognitive abilities in the sense just specified are thereby informants whom one can rely on, and *vice versa*. Closer inspection, however, reveals that first appearances are deceptive on this score. In order to see this, we just need to notice that it can be appropriate to rely on an informant who is forming her true belief via an unreliable cognitive ability, and also that it can be inappropriate to rely on an informant who nevertheless is forming a true belief via a reliable cognitive ability.

First, consider a potential informant who possesses a reliable cognitive ability as regards a certain subject matter but who is in an environment in which there exists a misleading defeater – one that you know about, but the prospective informant does not, and one that moreover you are unable to defeat. An example might be an informant who is a reliable barn detector, but where you have been given a misleading reason (e.g., false testimony from a good source) for supposing that the informant is in barn façade county. Given that this is a misleading defeater, the informant is in fact a *reliable* informant about the relevant subject matter. But given also that you know about the misleading defeater, and are aware that you are unable to defeat that defeater, would you be able to *rely on* this informant? Surely not.

The converse point also holds. In particular, we can imagine a case where there are compensating factors in play, known only to us, which mean that we can rely on the information presented to us by an informant even though this information is not the product of the informant's reliable cognitive abilities. Imagine, for example, an informant who thinks that they have a clairvoyant power to see into the future, but in fact is mistaken on this score (and we know this). Suppose further that we also know that this informant's wife is a very powerful person who wants her husband to continue to believe that he has this power and hence does what she can, where possible, to make sure that events turn out in the way that her husband predicts. Finally, suppose that we know that the informant's wife can fix the result of any horse race. With this knowledge in hand, the testimony of the informant regarding who will win tomorrow's horse race would certainly be information that one could rely on, even though the informant's true belief in this regard is in no way the product of a reliable cognitive ability.

In general, what is key to both of these kinds of cases is the role that luck is playing. In cases in which the informant's relevant cognitive abilities are reliable but where we are nonetheless unable to rely on the information she provides, the problem is that a dose of bad epistemic luck is cancelling out the good epistemic luck that our informant possesses the relevant reliable cognitive abilities (and thus is in this sense a good informant). In the case described above, for example, this bad epistemic luck is the presence of the undefeated misleading defeater. In contrast, in cases in which the informant lacks the relevant reliable cognitive abilities but is nonetheless providing us with information that we can rely on, a dose of good epistemic luck on our part is cancelling out the poor epistemic luck that our informant lacks the relevant reliable cognitive abilities (and thus is in this sense a bad informant). In the case described above, for example, this good epistemic luck is our knowledge of the compensating factors in play. With this point in mind, it ought to be clear why this ambiguity in the idea of a reliable informant explains why the concept of knowledge that evolves from the proto-concept of knowledge* will generate *both* the anti-luck and the ability intuition.

The idea is that as the range of cases which the proto-concept of knowledge* is meant to apply to widens, so too will a distinction open up between good informants who are reliable and good informants on whom we can rely. Accordingly, we would expect the concept of knowledge that results to respect *both* sides of this distinction. In particular, examples where an agent possesses the relevant reliable cognitive abilities but where the presence of epistemic luck means that we would not be able to rely on this agent *qua* informant would not be counted as cases of knowledge. (Consider the Barney case in this regard.) Similarly, cases in which an agent forms a true belief in an epistemically friendly environment – such that any true belief so formed would not be subject to epistemic luck – would not be counted as cases of knowledge so long as the agent concerned failed to exhibit the relevant reliable cognitive abilities in producing this safe cognitive success (even though we could rely on this agent *qua* informant). (Think of the Temp case in this regard.) In short, the concept of knowledge that results will both: (i) disallow cases of true belief as knowledge where the truth of the belief is substantively due to luck and hence unsafe, no matter what degree of cognitive ability is one display; and (ii) disallow cases of safe true belief as knowledge where the safe true belief isn't appropriately due to the exercise of the relevant cognitive abilities.

A very plausible and popular story about the genealogy of the concept of knowledge thus lends support to anti-luck virtue epistemology after all, despite first appearances. In fact, if I am right that the goal of picking out reliable informants is ambiguous in the way just described, then contrary to the prevailing wisdom on this score, this 'just so' account of the concept of knowledge actually *favours* anti-luck virtue epistemology over rival proposals, such as virtue epistemologies.

Concluding remarks

We have thus seen that there is an account of knowledge available – anti-luck virtue epistemology – which is able to deal with a wide range of problem cases in epistemology, and which, more importantly, is able to deal with those cases in a more satisfactory way than competing proposals. Moreover, we have seen that there is a sound diagnostic story available as to why knowledge should have the structure dictated by this proposal. There is thus good reason for supposing that anti-luck virtue epistemology is the right theory of knowledge to opt for.

Chapter summary

We began by reviewing the problems facing robust virtue epistemology and anti-luck epistemology, and relating them back to the question of how the anti-luck and ability intuitions relate to one another. We then explored a hybrid view, anti-luck virtue epistemology, which explicitly treats these two intuitions as imposing distinct constraints on a theory of knowledge. As we saw, it was important that this proposal was understood correctly, and in particular that it doesn't merely consist of the claim that knowledge has an independent anti-luck/safety condition and an ability/virtue condition. Rather what is required is a safe cognitive success that stands in a certain explanatory relationship to one's exercise of cognitive ability. The nature of this explanatory relationship was then explored, using the similar (though ultimately very different) explanatory relationship at issue in robust virtue epistemology as a foil. Anti-luck virtue epistemology was then 'tested' relative to a set of standard examples, and shown to be able to accommodate them. We saw that anti-luck virtue epistemology is compatible with both an epistemically internalist and an externalist rendering. We also considered the possibility that such an analysis of knowledge, while informative, might nonetheless fail to be reductive. Finally, we considered the question of why knowledge might have this two-aspect structure. One kind of motivation was offered in terms of the notion of *epistemic dependence*. A second motivation appealed to a popular *genealogical* account of the concept of knowledge.

Further introductory reading

See the further introductory readings listed for chapters 2 and 3, especially Turri & Sosa (2010) and Becker (2013).

Further advanced reading

See Pritchard, Millar & Haddock (2010, chs. 1–4) and Pritchard (2012a; 2015a) for a fuller defence of an anti-luck virtue epistemology. See Pritchard (*forthcoming b*) for a defence of the view in light of some recent objections. See Kallestrup & Pritchard (2013) for a defence of anti-luck virtue epistemology in the context of the notion of epistemic dependence. The genealogical story about the concept of knowledge discussed here was first offered by Craig (1991). For discussion of Craig's proposal, see B. Williams (2004) and Kusch (2009). See Greco (2008) for an example of an epistemologist who argues that this proposal lends support to robust virtue epistemology.

Free internet resources

See the free internet resources listed for chapters 2 and 3, especially Greco & Turri (2011).

Study questions

1. Try to restate, in your own words, why robust anti-luck epistemology is held to struggle to accommodate the ability intuition. Do you find this critique of robust anti-luck epistemology plausible?
2. Try to restate, in your own words, why robust virtue epistemology is held to struggle to accommodate the ability intuition. Do you find this critique of robust virtue epistemology plausible?
3. What is anti-luck virtue epistemology? In particular, why is this view not simply the claim that knowledge is composed of two completely independent conditions, safety and a virtue condition?
4. Explain in your own words how anti-luck virtue epistemology is meant to deal with cases like Temp.
5. Explain in your own words how anti-luck virtue epistemology is meant to deal with cases like Jenny.
6. Is anti-luck virtue epistemology a reductive account of knowledge? If not, does that matter?
7. What is epistemic dependence, and what does it mean to say that it comes in both a positive and a negative form?
8. Why might the source of the concept of knowledge be to flag reliable informants? What is the difference between the concept of knowledge and knowledge itself?

Sample essay questions

1. What is anti-luck virtue epistemology, and how does it differ from rival proposals? Is it successful as a theory of knowledge?
2. What, if anything, can reflecting on the practical purpose of the concept of knowledge tell us about knowledge itself?
3. 'A good analysis of knowledge need not be reductive.' Discuss.

5
Epistemic Externalism and Internalism

Introduction

At the end of chapter 1, we considered how the externalism/internalism distinction regarding knowledge is usually characterised. Recall that we defined this distinction in terms of whether one regarded an internal epistemic condition as being necessary for knowledge, where an internal epistemic condition is a condition that one can determine that one has satisfied by reflection alone. Typically, the internal epistemic condition in question is the justification condition, as it is conceived of in the classical theory of knowledge. Construed this way, the epistemic externalism/internalism distinction collapses into the question of whether one thinks that justification – i.e., the demand that one is able to offer good reflectively accessible reasons in support of one's belief – is necessary for knowledge. If one thinks that this is required for knowledge, then one is an epistemic internalist about knowledge. But if one thinks, at least sometimes anyway, that one can have knowledge while lacking a justification in this sense, then one is an epistemic externalist about knowledge.

In this chapter, we will look at this distinction in more detail, and offer a more nuanced description of it.

Three internalist theses

In digging a little deeper as regards the epistemic internalism/externalism distinction we need to consider some different ways in which the distinction gets characterised. In what follows, we will focus on the justification condition, internalistically construed, and ask what it is about justification on this construal that makes it an internalist epistemic condition. Henceforth, when I talk of 'justification', without qualification, it will be the internalist conception of justification that I have in mind.

As just noted, the standard construal of the epistemic externalist/internalist distinction holds that what makes justification an internal epistemic condition is that it is a condition which is reflectively accessible. We can define the general thesis in play here as follows:

Accessibilism
S's justification for believing a proposition is constituted solely by facts that S can know by reflection alone.

That is, whatever relevance non-reflectively accessible facts might have to the epistemic standing of a subject's belief, they can have no bearing, on this view, on the justification that the subject has for her belief.

What it means for a fact to be reflectively accessible is that the agent can come to know that fact simply by reflecting on the matter, and thus without having to make any further empirical inquiries. Note that 'reflection' here will usually involve introspection, *a priori* reasoning and memory of knowledge gained via either of these two sources. With this in mind, it ought to be clear why the justification condition satisfies the accessibilist rubric by epistemic internalist lights. After all, what it is to be justified is to have reasons available to the subject that speak in favour of the target proposition, where to be 'available' means that such reasons are easily citable by that subject. But if such reasons are citable in this way, and it is also the case that it is in virtue of possessing such reasons that one is justified, it seems to immediately follow that the justification condition, on the internalist view, satisfies accessibilism.

There are ways of strengthening or weakening this thesis, but for our purposes we can set this aside since our interest is in alternative, and possibly distinct, ways of drawing the epistemic externalism/internalism contrast. Consider the following thesis which some argue is instead distinctive of epistemic internalism:

Mentalism
S's justification for believing a proposition is constituted solely by S's mental states.

The guiding thought behind mentalism is that what makes you justified is restricted to your mental states, such as your beliefs and experiences, as opposed to extra-mental items, such as facts about the world (about the reliability of one's belief-forming processes, say).

On the face of it, accessibilism and mentalism are at least roughly extensionally equivalent, at least if we restrict our attention to simple non-inferential beliefs about the world around us (such as the perceptual belief that there is a chair in the room). With this restriction in play, it is plausible to suppose that there won't be a case of a belief that is justified in the sense demanded by accessibilism and yet unjustified in the sense demanded by mentalism, or a case of a belief that is justified in the sense demanded by mentalism and yet unjustified in the sense demanded by accessibilism. There is a good reason for this, in that it is natural to think that your epistemic basis for beliefs of this sort will essentially involve your mental states (e.g., your beliefs about the visual scene before you). A common view of mental states, however, is that they are by their nature the kind of thing that is reflectively accessible to one. Thus, it should not be surprising to learn that when it comes to justified beliefs of this sort the justification in question satisfies both the accessibilist and the mentalist rubric.

For example, a supporting reason that one might have for believing that there is a table before one could be that it seems to one as if there is a table there. But that it seems to one as if there is a table there is itself a fact about your mental states and hence, one might think, the kind of fact that is reflectively accessible. If that's right, then – at least if we confine our attentions to simple non-inferential beliefs about the world around us anyway (which we will be doing in what follows, to keep the discussion manageable) – mentalism and accessibilism stand or fall together as accounts of what makes the justification condition an internal epistemic condition.

Even if this is right, however, one can still legitimately ask the question as to which of these theses, if any, has the 'whip hand' when it comes to epistemic internalism. For example, while agreeing that mentalism and accessibilism are at least extensionally equivalent in the qualified sense just explained, some have nonetheless argued that mentalism is the more fundamental thesis to epistemic internalism. What they mean by this is that mentalism is the core thesis of epistemic internalism, with accessibilism a secondary, or derivative, thesis. We will return to this issue later.

There is also a third thesis that is often appealed to in discussions of epistemic internalism, albeit often not explicitly. In order to get a grip on what this thesis involves we need to first consider an intuition that is often said to be central to the case for epistemic internalism, in that it is meant to be an intuition that only epistemic internalists can accommodate. This is the so-called *new evil genius* intuition.

Consider the following case:

René
Poor René has been captured by mad scientists. They have removed his brain and placed it in a vat of nutrients in which it now floats, connected to a supercomputer by various wires. This supercomputer has wiped René's experiences of being abducted and now controls René's present experiences. In particular, the supercomputer ensures that René's experiences are pretty much the same as they were before, such that René continues to suppose that he is, for example, walking about his old environment, even though he is in fact merely a brain floating in a vat.

Now imagine a counterpart of René who has not been abducted and so really is going about his business as usual. Let us stipulate that the experiences being generated for René correspond to the experiences that René's counterpart is currently having, such that when René's counterpart has the experiences associated with, say, walking to work, René is 'fed' experiences as if he is walking to work too. René and his counterpart are thus having experiences that are indistinguishable (for them, at any rate). The new evil genius intuition is the claim that René's counterpart is no less justified in her beliefs than René is, given that their experiences are completely indistinguishable.

We thus get the following thesis:

The New Evil Genius Thesis
S's justification for believing a proposition is constituted solely by properties that S has in common with her envatted physical duplicate.

There is something very compelling about the new evil genius thesis, since there does seem a strong urge to say that these two agents can't be epistemically different, even if they have the misfortune (unbeknownst to them, of course) to be in very different situations. Indeed, insofar as epistemic internalism is wedded to mentalism and accessibilism, then there is a very natural explanation for this intuition. After all, intuitively at least, since one cannot distinguish between one's experiences and the parallel experiences one would have if one were one's envatted counterpart, there can't be anything reflectively accessible to one which is not available to one's counterpart. Similarly, there is reason to think that you share the same mental states as your envatted counterpart. After all, if there is no subjective difference between your experiences and the experiences of your counterpart – in the sense that you can't distinguish between the two sets of experiences – then it is natural to suppose that, in this regard at least, your mental states are essentially the same as your envatted counterpart's. For example, for both of you the way the world appears is exactly the same. If this right, then we thus have three different characterisations of epistemic internalism that may well be extensionally equivalent (at least provided, remember, we restrict our attentions to simple non-inferential beliefs about the world around us). Still, even if they do turn out to be equivalent in this way, it may nonetheless be the case that one of these characterisations is conceptually more fundamental, in the sense that it is the thesis which best characterises epistemic internalism.

Classical *versus* non-classical epistemic internalism

We will call *classical epistemic internalism* the view that endorses all three of the theses just set out, regardless of which of these theses, if any, it treats as more fundamental. In contrast, a *non-classical epistemic internalism* would be any view that accepts at least one of these theses but also denies at least one of these theses too (note that we will give a more refined characterisation of this position below). Is any non-classical view plausible?

One issue in this regard is whether one endorses *content externalism* (sometimes known as *semantic externalism*). Content externalists hold that mental content (e.g., the content of one thoughts) is determined, at least in part, by environmental factors. For example, a content externalist might hold that the contents of one's thoughts about a natural kind term like 'water' are dependent upon the chemical structure of water. Consider the following example:

Hilary
Hilary lives on a far-off planet that is much the same as earth. On this planet there is a clear, odourless liquid that is indistinguishable from water, and that is used in just the same way on this planet as we use water (e.g., people bathe in it, make drinks from it, and so on). Like us, the people on Hilary's planet call this liquid 'water'. Crucially, however, the chemical structure of the 'water' liquid on Hilary's planet is not H_2O but XYZ.

According to one version of content externalism at any rate, when Hilary thinks about the substance that she calls 'water' she is not having a thought with the same content as we would have if we thought a parallel thought about what we call 'water'. For what Hilary is thinking about is a different substance entirely – water*, say, rather than water – one that has a chemical structure of XYZ rather than H_2O.

We do not need to get into the issue of whether content externalism (in some form) is true here, since all that matters for our purposes is that this is a widely accepted thesis in philosophy which has important ramifications for how we are understanding the three formulations of epistemic internalism just noted. In particular, if content externalism is true, then there is every reason for thinking that these three formulations of epistemic internalism are not extensionally equivalent after all, even in the restricted sense outlined above.

In particular, any epistemic internalist who subscribes to content externalism and either mentalism or accessibilism will tend to be suspicious of the new evil genius thesis. After all, given content externalism, that two subjects (i.e., oneself and one's envatted counterpart) are undergoing indistinguishable mental states need not mean that they are the same mental states (i.e., mental states with the same content). Hilary and his counterpart on earth, after all, although they seem to have identical mental lives, are nonetheless – unbeknownst to them – thinking thoughts about what they both call 'water' that have very different contents. Couldn't something similar be happening as regards oneself and one's envatted duplicate? Relatedly, given content externalism, that two subjects are undergoing indistinguishable mental states need not mean that the same set of facts is reflectively accessible to them. Hilary and his counterpart on earth are undergoing indistinguishable mental states, and yet there is a different set of facts reflectively accessible to them (one set of facts which includes thoughts about water, and another set of facts which includes thoughts about water*). Again, couldn't something similar be happening as regards oneself and one's envatted duplicate?

Rather than granting that content externalism leads to a non-classical version of epistemic internalism, one could instead appeal to a distinction that philosophers of language sometimes draw between 'narrow' and 'broad' mental content. This distinction is controversial, and in particular it is controversial just how one should draw it. Very roughly, whereas broad mental content is dependent upon features of the subject's environment (i.e., in addition to being dependent upon features of the individual herself), narrow mental content is not dependent upon the subject's environment. Content externalism is thus the view that at least some mental content is broad mental content. Even so, insofar as we grant content externalism and can make sense of the distinction between broad and narrow mental content, we could argue that the kind of mental content that is of interest to the epistemic internalist is specifically narrow mental content. If that's right, then one could preserve a classical epistemic internalism even while granting content externalism. For although it may follow from content externalism that one differs from one's envatted counterpart in terms of the mental states and the facts to which one has reflective access, nonetheless this difference disappears once we exclusively focus upon narrow mental content. In this way, we could in principle make the new evil genius thesis once more line up alongside accessibilism and mentalism. Moreover, if this could be done then one could motivate the exclusive emphasis on narrow mental content by arguing that it is the only way of preserving the triad of theses that constitute classical epistemic internalism. Accordingly, it must be the case that what epistemic internalists are really interested in is narrow mental content rather than broad mental content.

Rather than evaluate the prospects of this way of reconciling content externalism with classical epistemic internalism, we will instead explore a specific proposal in epistemology which is usually characterised as an epistemically internalist thesis but which does not subscribe to all three versions of epistemic internalism we have identified. This position is known as *epistemological disjunctivism*.

Epistemological disjunctivism

What is central to epistemological disjunctivism is the claim that at least some reasons are both *factive*, where this means that the reason entails the proposition that it is a reason for, and *reflectively accessible*. An example of a factive reason is that one *sees that p*, since one can only see that *p* provided that *p* is true. For instance, I can only see that John is wearing a red jumper if he is indeed wearing a red jumper. In contrast, if it is not true that John is wearing a red jumper, then at best I can merely *seem to see* that this is the case (and note that seeming to see that *p*, unlike seeing that *p*, is non-factive). In what follows we will take seeing that *p* to be our paradigm case of a factive reason. The key claim made by epistemological disjunctivism, then, is that in suitable conditions an agent's reason for believing a proposition can be that she sees that *p*, and that this reason can be reflectively accessible to her. Epistemological disjunctivism thus seems to be committed to a form of accessibilism, at least as regards this particular kind of belief, while also endorsing factive reasons.

According to classical internalism, this combination of theses is not possible. After all, whether one is in a situation in which one sees that *p* as opposed to merely seeming to see that *p* (as, for instance, when one is deceived in some way) need not be something that the agent is able to reflectively distinguish. For example, suppose that I am in excellent cognitive conditions and so see that there is a table before me. According to epistemological disjunctivism, that I see that there is a table before me can form part of my rational support for believing that there is a table before me. Nonetheless, it is entirely conceivable that my envatted counterpart is presently undergoing experiences that are subjectively indistinguishable from the experiences I have, and hence also takes himself to see that there is a table before him. But since there is no table before my rational counterpart, it follows that he cannot see that there is a table before him, and hence this cannot form part of his rational support for believing that there is a table before him. Hence, if epistemological disjunctivism is true, then the rational standing of my belief, and thus the justification I have for this belief, is very different – and significantly better than – the rational standing, and thus justification, that my envatted counterpart has for his belief (indeed, if his belief is justified at all). But that means that epistemological disjunctivism, while endorsing accessibilism (at least as regards this particular kind of belief anyway), is clearly committed to rejecting the new evil genius thesis, as I am now epistemically better off than my envatted counterpart.

Epistemological disjunctivism is thus a non-classical version of epistemic internalism to the extent that it rejects the new evil genius thesis. That leaves mentalism. Here one might think that there is no in-principle conflict with factive reasons. After all, such reasons describe an experiential mental state – e.g., the experiential mental state of seeing that *p*. Thus, in a case in which two agents with subjectively indistinguishable experiences are nonetheless in possession of different reasons (factive and non-factive, respectively) – as in the case of oneself and one's envatted duplicate – the difference in justificatory standing exhibited by these two agents is accounted for by the fact that they have, unbeknownst to them, different mental states. So in principle one could regard epistemological disjunctivism as being compatible with mentalism.

Still, just as we saw in our discussion of content externalism in the last section, one might respond to epistemological disjunctivism by arguing that we should preserve classical epistemic internalism by clarifying how we are understanding the three internalist theses in question. For example, one might argue that mentalism is really a thesis about our non-factive mental states, such that insofar as we do have factive mental states, they are not within the scope of this thesis. One could then argue that one's mental states and the mental states of one's envatted counterpart are alike in the relevant respects, in that they both concern the non-factive mental state of seeming to see that p. So long as one makes a similar restriction to how one understands the new evil genius thesis, then mentalism and the new evil genius thesis can thus be made to square with the existence of factive mental states.

The difficult issue here will be how to square accessibilism with mentalism and the new evil genius thesis, even on the new rendering. After all, epistemological disjunctivism is specifically characterised in terms of the claim that these factive reasons are reflectively accessible. Presumably, then, the proponent of classical internalism will have to maintain that this combination of theses is simply untenable, to the extent that either the reasons are factive, in which case they aren't reflectively accessible, or else they are genuinely reflectively accessible, in which case they aren't factive. With this point in mind, let's look a bit more closely at whether the idea of factive reflectively accessible reasons is even coherent.

Reflectively accessible factive reasons

Here's one way of stating the kind of concern the classical epistemic internalist will have about factive reflectively accessible reasons. For how can one have reflective access to a factive reason given that whether or not one's reason is a factive reason rather than a corresponding non-factive reason – e.g., a seeing that p rather than a mere seeming to see that p – depends upon facts in the world that one has (it seems) no reflective access to? In short, the worry is that what makes a reason factive as opposed to non-factive are environmental, and thus not reflectively accessible, factors. Accordingly, one might naturally hold that you and your deceived counterpart must have the same reflectively accessible reasons, and thus that the reasons you have access to are always non-factive reasons. This means that whether or not you do in fact see that p, your reason for believing that p can be no better than that you seem to see that p.

The argument in play here goes something like as follows, where the 'good case' is a case in which you see that p, and the 'bad' case is a corresponding (and indistinguishable) case in which p is false and so it cannot be the case that you see that p (such as a case in which one is envatted):

The Argument Against Reflectively Accessible Factive Reasons
(1) In the bad case, the justificatory support that one has for one's belief that p can be no better than that one seems to see that p.
(2) *Ex hypothesi*, the experiences one has in the good case are indistinguishable from the experiences one has in the bad case.
(C) So, in the good case, the justificatory support that one has for one's belief that p can be no better than that one seems to see that p.

Epistemological disjunctivists, however, explicitly argue that factive reasons can be reflectively accessible, and hence must reject this argument. But where do they claim that this argument goes wrong?

Well, the problematic step seems to be from (2) to (C). After all, remember that epistemological disjunctivists reject the new evil genius thesis. Indeed, they explicitly argue that two agents with indistinguishable experiences can nonetheless differ in terms of the reflectively accessible rational support available to them. But with this thesis denied, it is far from clear how (C) is meant to follow from (2), since why otherwise should the fact that the experiences in the two cases are indistinguishable entail that there is no difference in justificatory standing (such that the justificatory standing in the good case is no better than it is in the bad case)? If that's right, then it is open to the epistemological disjunctivist to use their denial of the new evil genius thesis to resist this argument and thereby maintain accessibilism and mentalism. This combination of theses would certainly constitute a *bona fide* version of epistemic internalism, albeit a non-classical version.

That there is the logical space to argue for such a position does not mean that the view is plausible, however, since there are other *prima facie* problems for such a proposal to deal with. Rather than run through them all, however, which would take us too far afield, we will instead just rehearse one key problem and look at how epistemological disjunctivism deals with it. This is the problem of showing how epistemological disjunctivism is to avoid the implication that we are able to come to know facts about the environment by reflection alone. For example, suppose I have reflective access to the fact that I see that p, and that I also know *a priori* that seeing that p entails p. Doesn't that mean that I am in a position to infer, on purely reflective grounds, that p is true? If that's right, then it seems that I can come to know that, for example, there is a table in front of me purely through a process of introspection and inference, and that looks highly problematic.

In outline, epistemological disjunctivism responds to this problem by pointing out that although one has reflective access to factive reasons, it does not follow that the reasons themselves are non-empirical. In fact, they are explicitly empirical reasons, of a perceptual kind. Moreover, on this view one only has reflective access to this rational support insofar as one has empirical knowledge of the target proposition. Accordingly, it follows that there could be no route to non-empirical knowledge of the target environmental proposition, since in order to be in a position to have reflective access to the relevant factive reason, one would already need to have empirical knowledge of the target proposition.

What is interesting about a proposal like epistemological disjunctivism, assuming it can be made plausible (i.e., that it can avoid fatal objections), is that it offers a distinctive epistemological pay-off. For notice that the view marries two key components of standard internalist and externalist theses in epistemology. On the one hand, it demands that one's rational support be reflectively accessible and so avoids the problem faced by epistemic externalists of making such epistemic support opaque to one. On the other hand, however, it also allows that one's rational support – some of it at any rate – can have a direct relationship to how the world in fact is, something that simply seems impossible on classical internalist views.

One final point about epistemological disjunctivism that is worth remarking upon is its relationship to other proposals in the theory of knowledge that we have considered, such as anti-luck and virtue (and mixed) epistemologies. Is endorsing epistemological disjunctivism compatible with also endorsing one of these proposals? The first thing to notice here is that epistemological disjunctivism is primarily concerned with a very specific claim – *viz.*, that in paradigm cases of perceptual knowledge, one can be in possession of reflectively accessible factive reasons in support of one's belief. In principle, one can combine this kind of claim with any number of views about the nature of knowledge in general, since epistemological disjunctivism isn't a thesis about knowledge in general, but only about a particular variety of knowledge. So, for example, perhaps knowledge in general should be understood along the lines suggested by anti-luck virtue epistemology, but paradigm cases of perceptual knowledge should be understood along the lines proposed by epistemological disjunctivism. All one needs to do to make the two compatible is to tell a plausible story about how possession of reflectively accessible factive reasons can meet the epistemic rubric laid down by anti-luck virtue epistemology, but that should be relatively straightforward. After all, if one is in possession of a factive reason in support of one's perceptual belief – something which, recall, one only has in paradigmatic perceptual conditions – then how could one's belief fail to satisfy the rubric laid down by anti-luck virtue epistemology?

More generally, notice that the three theses that we saw above to be characteristic of epistemic internalism were all about the nature of (internalist) justification. Accordingly, in endorsing, say, accessibilism about justification, epistemological disjunctivism is not thereby committing itself to internalism about knowledge (which, recall, is the idea that knowledge entails internalist justification, or at least something in that general vicinity). So one could endorse epistemological disjunctivism and, thereby, perhaps also accessibilism about justification (at least as regards paradigm cases of perceptual belief), but nonetheless maintain that sometimes knowledge is possessed in the absence of reflectively accessible reasons, factive or otherwise. In this way, one could be an epistemic internalist about (paradigm cases of) perceptual knowledge, for example, but be an epistemic externalist about knowledge in general, in that one does not hold that all knowledge entails internalist justification.

In any case, the upshot of all this is that the epistemological externalism/internalism distinction is multiply complex. The very nature of the kind of theses that characterise the commitments of epistemic internalism/externalism is contentious. In addition, the extent to which one is committed to these theses in virtue of being an epistemic internalist/externalist – in particular, whether one holds that satisfying them is necessary for knowledge – is also contentious. This means that rather than a polar opposition between two monolithic views – epistemic externalism *versus* epistemic internalism – we should instead expect a spectrum of different positions that embody characteristic epistemic internalist or externalist commitments to various extents.

Chapter summary

We looked at three theses that are characteristically associated with epistemic internalism. The first was *accessibilism*, which is roughly the view that one's internalist justification consists in having reflective access to the relevant facts. The second was *mentalism*, which is roughly the view that internalist justification is solely constituted by one's mental states. The third was the *new evil demon thesis*, which is roughly the view that internalist justification is solely constituted by the properties that one has in common with one's envatted counterpart. With these three theses in play we can distinguish between a *classical epistemic internalism*, which adheres to all three, and a *non-classical epistemic internalism*, which rejects at least one of these theses (and at most two). We saw that one ground for offering a non-classical form of epistemic internalism is *content externalism*. Very roughly, content externalism holds that mental content can be determined, at least in part, by environmental factors that are external to the subject. One consequence of this proposal is that one might well not be thinking thoughts with the same content as one's envatted counterpart, even though one's experiences are subjectively indistinguishable. That opens up the possibility that accessibilism and mentalism might come apart from the new evil demon thesis. We considered one way of bringing them back together, even while granting the truth of content externalism, which was to make these theses characterising epistemic internalism explicitly about *narrow mental content* (as opposed to *broad mental content*). A second potential form of non-classical epistemic internalism is *epistemological disjunctivism*. This holds that in paradigm cases of perceptual knowledge, one's rational support can consist of reflectively accessible factive reasons. In particular, it can consist of the reflectively accessible rational support that one *sees that p* (which entails p). While epistemological disjunctivism is compatible with accessibilism and mentalism, it explicitly disavows the new evil demon thesis. In particular, epistemological disjunctivism holds that although one's experiences are indistinguishable from the experiences of one's envatted counterpart, it is nonetheless the case that the rational support one's beliefs enjoy can be very different to that enjoyed by one's counterpart's beliefs (i.e., where one has factive rational support for one's beliefs, unlike one's envatted duplicate). We noted that this proposal is highly controversial, and we considered one particular objection to the view, and looked at how proponents of epistemological disjunctivism respond to this objection. Finally, we related this discussion back to the more general issue of how to understand the epistemic externalism/internalism distinction, and noted how there is potentially a whole spectrum of intermediate positions available between a classical epistemic internalism on the one hand and a classical epistemic externalism (e.g., process reliabilism) on the other hand.

Further introductory reading

For a useful annotated bibliography on epistemic justification, which covers the epistemic externalism and internalism distinction in some depth, see Graham (2011). For a helpful annotated bibliography of writings on content externalism, see Goldberg (2010). See also Poston (2008)

90 *Epistemology*

and Pappas (2014), which are also listed below under 'free internet resources'.

Further advanced reading

For a good collection of essays on the epistemic externalism/internalism distinction, see Kornblith (2001). For an excellent overview of content externalism, see Kallestrup (2011). The key discussion of the new evil genius intuition is Lehrer & Cohen (1983). The classic defence of mentalism can be found in Conee & Feldman (2004). For a key recent defence of epistemological disjunctivism, see Pritchard (2012b), which draws on earlier work by McDowell (e.g., 1995). Note that, just as one can delineate potential non-classical versions of epistemic internalism, so one can delineate potential non-classical versions of epistemic externalism as well (i.e., in terms of how they accept some, but not all, the theses that are usually characteristic of epistemic externalism). See Pritchard (2011) for an explanation of how Williamson's (2000) knowledge-first epistemology could be thought of as a non-classical version of epistemic externalism. And see Gibbons (2006) for a distinctive version of 'access' *ex*ternalism.

Free internet resources

For two excellent overview of the epistemic externalism/internalism distinction, see Poston (2008) and Pappas (2014). For a useful overview of content externalism, see Lau & Deutsch (2014). See also Smith (2013).

Study questions

1. What is accessibilism? Why might this thesis be characteristic of epistemic internalism?
2. What is mentalism? How, if at all, does it differ from accessibilism? Why might this thesis be characteristic of epistemic internalism?
3. What is the new evil genius thesis? How does this thesis relate to accessibilism and mentalism? Why might this thesis be characteristic of epistemic internalism?
4. Try to state, in your own words, what content externalism is. How might this thesis lead one into rejecting the new evil genius thesis?
5. What is narrow mental content, and how might this notion allow one to combine content externalism with classical epistemic internalism?
6. What is epistemological disjunctivism? Explain why epistemological disjunctivism is committed to accessibilism (at least as regards

paradigm instances of perceptual knowledge), but rejects the new evil genius thesis.
7 How plausible do you find the suggestion that there could be reflectively accessible factive reasons? What kinds of problems do you think this proposal might face?

Sample essay questions
1 What is the epistemic internalist conception of justification? Does knowledge entail justification, as the internalist conceives of this notion?
2 Why might content externalism lead one to embrace a non-classical form of epistemic internalism, which rejects the new evil genius thesis? Is there a way of reconciling content externalism with classical epistemic internalism?
3 Could one's perceptual beliefs ever enjoy reflectively accessible rational support that is also factive (i.e., which entails the truth of the belief in question)?

6
Radical Scepticism

Introduction

Radical scepticism is the view that knowledge – most of it at any rate – is impossible. Strictly speaking it is not really a view, in that while there have historically been some people who have proposed such a position, its philosophical interest does not rest on whether there are any actual sceptics. The reason for this is that, properly expressed, radical scepticism is meant to be a *paradox*, in that it exposes a deep tension in our own epistemological concepts. Like all paradoxes, radical scepticism proceeds by identifying a series of claims that we would individually take to be highly intuitive, but which are shown to collectively entail an intellectually unacceptable conclusion – in this instance that knowledge is impossible. Since paradoxes are generated by our own concepts – in this case our epistemological concepts – it clearly doesn't matter whether there is anyone out there who actually argues for the sceptical conclusion since it would still constitute a serious philosophical problem that we would need to deal with even if this were not the case.

One more point about radical scepticism that is worthy of note before we get into the nitty-gritty of the problem is just how radical a challenge it poses. For notice that the claim is not simply that we don't in fact have a significant amount of knowledge, but rather that it would be *impossible* for us to have a significant amount of knowledge. The former claim, while no doubt intellectually devastating to a certain degree, is not nearly so philosophically interesting. After all, this thesis leaves it open that if only we were cleverer, or more observant, or more careful in how we formed our beliefs (etc.), then we would have lots of knowledge after all. The radical sceptical claim, however, is precisely that, no matter how clever or observant or conscientious (etc.) we are, we will never have a significant amount of knowledge. That is a disturbing claim indeed.

The closure-based radical sceptical argument

One influential way of motivating radical scepticism involves a very simple argument with just two premises. The first premise is the claim that we are unable to know the denials of sceptical hypotheses. Sceptical hypotheses are scenarios in which one's experiences are subjectively indistinguishable from one's normal experiences, but where one's beliefs are radically error. Consider, for example, the René case that we came across in chapter 5. Recall that René had had his brain removed and placed in a vat of nutrients to keep it alive. While in this vat it was connected to electrodes to stimulate it to have subjectively indistinguishable experiences from the experiences René would have had if he had not been abducted.

Here is the question: how does one know that one is not in the same situation as René right now? In particular, imagine that you have a counterpart who has been envatted in this way and hence is being 'fed' experiences just like the experiences that you are presently having. For example, while I am in fact typing on my laptop just now and having experiences which indicate this (e.g., the feel of the keyboard on my fingers, the visual impression of the laptop screen before me, and so on), my envatted counterpart is having experiences which are, it seems, essentially the same (indeed, depending on your view of what constitutes an experience, in virtue of being indistinguishable they may even qualify as being the *same* experiences). Crucially, however, while my experiences are offering me a guide to how the world in fact is, my envatted counterpart's experiences are no guide at all as to the nature of his environment, since his experiences are all being faked. Call this sceptical hypothesis involving brains in vats the *BIV sceptical hypothesis*, and call anyone who is the victim of such a hypothesis a *BIV*.

The problem posed by sceptical hypotheses is that since they involve experiences that are indistinguishable from normal non-sceptical experiences, it seems that one can never know that one is not the victim of a sceptical hypothesis. Right now, for example, I take it as given that I really am typing this chapter on my laptop, but given that I would have experiences which were exactly alike if I were envatted, how can I possibly know that I am not in fact envatted just now and merely seeming to be typing this chapter on my laptop? The first premise of this sceptical argument is thus that I cannot know that sceptical hypotheses, such as the BIV sceptical hypothesis, are false.

Notice that this claim in itself is not enough to motivate the sceptical conclusion that we know next to nothing, since one natural response to the presentation of a sceptical hypothesis is to say that it doesn't matter to most of our knowledge whether or not one can rule it out. That is, in order to know that, say, I am typing on my computer just now I only need to rule out serious error possibilities, and not far-fetched ones like the BIV sceptical hypothesis.

On the face of it, this seems a very plausible way of responding to sceptical hypotheses since it seems to accord with our usual epistemic practices when it comes to error possibilities. For example, suppose that I am told by a reliable informant that I may have ingested some drugs which would prompt very vivid hallucinations. Clearly, I am now unable to take my experiences at face value and must instead make independent checks on what I see. Only then can I gain knowledge that I am typing on my computer. Sceptical hypotheses are not like error possibilities of this sort, however, in that we have no specific reason to think that we might be, say, a BIV as we do to think that we might be hallucinating in the case just described. After all, given that your experiences are exactly like what they would be were one not to be a victim of a sceptical hypothesis, then what specific reason could there be for one to believe that a sceptical hypothesis might be true? And where we have no specific reason for believing that a certain error possibility might obtain, our normal practice is simply to disregard it. Indeed, imagine that one had no specific reason for thinking that one has recently ingested drugs which induce very vivid hallucinations. Does one then even have to rule out this error possibility before one can know that one is typing on one's computer? Intuitively, one does not. And yet it would appear that this is the situation we are in as regards the sceptical hypotheses more generally, and hence it seems that we ought to be able to disregard them with impunity too.

The general thought in play here is what is known as the *relevant alternatives intuition* about knowledge: that in order to have knowledge one only needs to be able to rule out relevant error possibilities (i.e. alternatives), and not also the irrelevant ones. And what makes an alternative relevant? Well, intuitively at least, it is whether there is any specific reason for thinking that it is the kind of error possibility that could well obtain.

The radical sceptic thus needs a further premise that can make our inability to rule out the sceptical error possibilities have a bearing on our knowledge of ordinary propositions, such as my knowledge that I am presently typing on a laptop. One way of doing this would be to argue for *infallibilism*, which is the thesis that *all* error possibilities must be ruled out before one can possess knowledge. There are some grounds in favour of infallibilism. Some have argued, for example, that knowledge requires certainty, and certainty requires infallibilism. Infallibilism is, however, clearly a highly contentious thesis (it is certainly in conflict with the relevant alternatives intuition). Accordingly, if there is a way of motivating radical scepticism without making an appeal to this thesis, then that will be preferable from the sceptic's point of view. As we will now see, there is.

In particular, all the sceptic needs is a very intuitive principle known as the *closure principle*. This principle states that knowledge is 'closed' under known entailment, in the sense that if one knows one proposition, and one knows that this proposition entails a second proposition, then one knows that second proposition. Stated more formally:

The Closure Principle
If an agent, S, knows a proposition, p, and knows that p entails a second proposition, q, then S knows that q.

So expressed, the closure principle seems utterly uncontentious. If, for example, you know that you are presently seated, and you know that if you are presently seated then you are not presently standing, then surely you also know that you are not presently standing. What could be more intuitive than that?

The problem posed by the closure principle, however, is that there are lots of 'everyday' propositions – i.e., propositions which (or so we think at any rate) we straightforwardly know, such as my putative knowledge that I am currently sitting at my office desk in Edinburgh – which entail the denial of sceptical hypotheses. Given the closure principle, however, it follows that if we do indeed know these propositions, then we must also be in a position to know the denials of sceptical hypotheses as well. Conversely, if the sceptic is right that we are unable to know the denials of sceptical hypotheses, then it seems that we cannot know these everyday propositions either.

To illustrate this point, consider a concrete example. If I know anything right now, then I surely know that I have two hands. But notice that BIVs by definition don't have hands. Hence, if I do know that I have two hands then, given that the closure principle holds (and given that I know that if I have two hands, then I'm not a BIV), it follows that I must know that I'm not a BIV. But, *ex hypothesi*, it is impossible to know that I am not a BIV, and hence it must be the case that I don't know that I've got two hands either. But what goes here for having hands goes for an awful lot of what we think we know, since most everyday propositions are inconsistent with at least one sceptical hypothesis (one would just need to vary the sceptical hypothesis to suit).

We are now in a position to formulate our sceptical argument.

The Closure-Based Sceptical Argument
(1) It is impossible to know the denials of sceptical hypotheses.
(2) If we have a significant amount of knowledge of everyday propositions, then we must be able to know the denials of (at least some) sceptical hypotheses.
(C) So, we don't have a significant amount of knowledge of everyday propositions (indeed, such knowledge is *impossible*).

The first premise is just meant to follow from the nature of sceptical hypotheses. The second premise is meant to follow from the closure principle. But with both premises in play the radical sceptical conclusion becomes irresistible. Given that the first premise is highly intuitive, and the second principle is also highly intuitive once we recognise that it follows immediately from the highly plausible closure principle, we have a paradox on our hands, in that we have highly intuitive premises generating a highly counterintuitive conclusion.

Responding to the closure-based sceptical argument I: denial of the closure principle

One might think that the weakest point in this argument is its dependence on the closure principle, and thus that once we recognise that this principle generates this sceptical conclusion, this is a decisive ground on which to reject it. This is easier said than done, however.

The most influential way of objecting to the closure principle is by appealing to the sensitivity principle that we considered in chapter 2. We noted there that there are some problems with this principle, and we argued that the safety principle was ultimately preferable as a means of capturing the anti-luck condition. For now, however, we will set these difficulties to one side and explore why adopting the sensitivity principle might give one grounds to reject the closure principle.

Recall how we formulated the sensitivity principle in chapter 2.

The Sensitivity Principle
If S knows that *p*, then *S*'s true belief that *p* is such that, had *p* been false, S would not have believed *p*.

Stated informally, the sensitivity principle demands that one's true belief be such that, in the nearest possible worlds in which what one believes is no longer true, one no longer believes the target proposition. So, for example, my true belief that I have two hands is sensitive because, in the nearest possible worlds in which I don't have hands – where I am staring incredulously at stumps at the ends of my arms right now – I no longer believe that I have hands (hands are the kind of thing, we might say, which are conspicuous by their absence). In general, for most of the everyday propositions that we believe it is fairly easy to have a sensitive belief in these propositions. Hence, a sensitivity-based epistemology will be inclined to credit us with knowledge of these everyday propositions.

Interestingly, however, it seems that our beliefs in the denials of sceptical hypotheses are by definition *insensitive*. After all, since there is no way of determining that one is not the victim of a sceptical hypothesis, it follows that were one to be the victim of such an error possibility, one would continue to believe in the denial of that sceptical hypothesis regardless. Take the BIV hypothesis, for example. Right now I believe that I am not a BIV, and this belief is, let us grant, true. Crucially, however, in the nearest possible worlds in which it is no longer true that I am not a BIV (i.e., the worlds in which I am a BIV) I will continue to believe that I'm not a BIV regardless since my experiences will be indistinguishable from my current experiences. My belief in this proposition is thus insensitive, in that the relevant fact can change, but my belief wouldn't change with it.

One advantage of the sensitivity principle is thus that it can account for why we regard the first premise of the sceptical argument as so compelling. According to a sensitivity-based epistemology, that is, one lacks knowledge of the denials of sceptical hypotheses precisely because it is impossible to have a sensitive belief in this regard. Notice, however, that we have already granted that our beliefs in everyday propositions are typically sensitive, and hence there is no problem (on this score at least) with supposing that we do know an awful lot of what we think we know. This fact has prompted some proponents of a sensitivity-based epistemology to argue for the rejection of the closure principle, and thus for the rejection of the second premise in the sceptical argument as well. In particular, they argue that what the sensitivity principle illustrates is that we can have knowledge of everyday propositions even while lacking knowledge of the denials of sceptical hypotheses, and hence that the closure principle must be rejected.

Given the plausibility of the closure principle, it is incumbent upon anyone who takes this anti-sceptical line to offer an adequate diagnostic story to explain why such a principle can be both highly plausible and yet also false. Let us grant, for the sake of argument, that there are compelling diagnostic stories available to sensitivity-based theorists in this regard. Even granted this supposition, ought we to find this approach to the sceptical problem feasible?

I think not. Part of the worry here concerns the more general problems facing the sensitivity principle that we noted in chapter 2. In particular, we noted there that the safety principle seems far more preferable as an anti-luck principle than the sensitivity principle. Crucially, however, the safety principle isn't obviously in conflict with the closure principle at all. Consider first one's belief that one has two hands. In order for this to be safe one needs it to be the case that in all near-by possible worlds – certainly most near-by possible worlds at any rate, and all very close near-by possible worlds – in which one forms a belief in this proposition, this belief is true. In order for this condition to be met, it is clearly essential that sceptical possible worlds – i.e., possible worlds in which sceptical hypotheses are true – are modally far off, since otherwise there would be a near-by possible world in which one forms a false belief about this proposition, such as the worlds in which one is a (handless) BIV. Given that the sceptical possible worlds are indeed modally far off, however, then it ought to be clear that one's belief that one is not the victim of a sceptical hypothesis will also be safe as well. After all, it will be true, and since there are no near-by possible worlds in which sceptical hypotheses obtain, there will be no near-by possible world in which one forms this belief and one's belief is false. So on this score at least, insofar as one has knowledge of everyday propositions, then there is no reason to think that one lacks knowledge of the denials of sceptical hypotheses, and hence no basis (on this score at least) to deny the closure principle.

Accordingly, if one is persuaded by the more general problems facing the sensitivity principle and hence opts for the safety principle as one's anti-luck principle of choice as a result, then that would preclude one from taking the anti-sceptical line of denying the closure principle on the grounds offered by proponents of the sensitivity principle (though it does open up a new anti-sceptical line, as we will see in a moment). There are also independent concerns about using the sensitivity principle to reject the closure principle. In particular, it isn't clear that when the sensitivity principle is properly understood it does generate the sceptical counterexamples to this principle that it is supposed to.

Recall that we noted in chapter 2 that the sensitivity principle needs to be understood as relativized to the belief-forming method actually employed if is to avoid generating some counterintuitive consequences. We also noted, however, that what constitutes one's belief-forming method needs to be understood *externalistically* in the sense that what counts is what in fact gave rise to your belief and not (which could be different) what you believe gave rise to your belief. The problem, however, is that if we read the sensitivity principle this way, such that we only consider the nearest possible worlds in which one forms one's belief in the same way as one does in the actual world, then it isn't clear that our beliefs in the denials of sceptical hypotheses are fated to be insensitive.

We can illustrate this by considering the BIV sceptical hypothesis. Suppose that one does have knowledge – and thus a sensitive belief – that one has two hands. The actual world is thus not a world in which a sceptical hypothesis obtains, nor does any such hypothesis obtain in any of the nearest possible worlds to the actual world. Now suppose that one forms one's belief that one is not a BIV. Presumably, what gives rise to this belief is a mixture of perception and inference. That is, one perceives that the world is a certain way, and one infers on this basis that the BIV sceptical hypothesis is false. This belief is true, but is it sensitive now that we are relativizing sensitivity to the actual way in which one forms one's belief? Well, in order to answer this question we need to consider the nearest possible world in which one is a BIV and consider whether one continues to believe that one is not a BIV in this world *on the same basis as in the actual world* (i.e., through a mixture of perception and inference). The trouble is, of course, that in the BIV world one does not perceive anything, and hence one's actual method of belief-formation is in fact unavailable. Moreover, note this is a general feature of sceptical hypotheses in that they all involve the agent forming beliefs in very different ways from how they would form those beliefs were the sceptical hypothesis not to obtain.

Hence it seems that once we formulate the sensitivity principle correctly, we are unable to get the clear counterexamples to the closure principle that were advertised as a ground for rejecting this principle. But given the great plausibility of the closure principle, and given also the other problems facing the sensitivity principle, this failure to generate a clear case for thinking that there are counterexamples to the closure principle is a pretty severe problem.

Responding to the closure-based sceptical argument II: attributer contextualism

If one allows the closure principle, however, then one must grant the second premise of the sceptical argument. Given that the argument is clearly valid, that means that the only other option available is to deny the first premise of the argument and thus maintain that one can know the denials of sceptical hypotheses after all. As we will see, there are two main ways of doing this.

The first way that we will consider involves an appeal to a contextualist thesis about 'knows'. According to this view, known as *attributer contextualism*, our use of this term is highly context-sensitive. In particular, different contexts pick out different epistemic standings that one needs to satisfy in order to be correctly said to know. Accordingly, while the assertion '*S* knows that *p*' may be true when asserted in one context where the epistemic standards in operation are very low, the very same sentence when asserted about the same subject and the same proposition (and with all other relevant factors, like *S*'s evidence, kept fixed) can be false when asserted in a different context where the epistemic standards are more demanding.

Let's consider an example to see how this proposal would work. The idea is that in normal situations very undemanding epistemic standards are in operation. Suppose that you are in such a context right now (as we will see in a moment, according to the attributer contextualist this is in fact unlikely to be the case). Now suppose that you assert, taking into account what you know about me, the following sentence: 'Duncan knows that he has two hands'. Given that the epistemic standards in operation in your context are low, this assertion ought to come out as true. But given the closure principle, which the attributer contextualist doesn't deny, this means that I must also be in a position to know that I am not a BIV too (at least if I know the relevant entailment).

But why, then, do we think that it is *impossible* to know that one is not a BIV? Well, the attributer contextualist explanation for this is that in contexts in which radical sceptical hypotheses are under consideration, the epistemic standards in operation are much more demanding than in normal contexts. Thus it follows that any assertion of 'Duncan knows that he is not a BIV' will express a falsehood, since it will, by definition, be asserted relative to a context in which radical sceptical hypotheses are under consideration and thus where the epistemic standards in operation are very high. Notice, however, that allowing this much does not create any tension with the closure principle since, relative to this context, one will not know that one has two hands either (i.e., any assertion in this context of 'Duncan knows that he has two hands' will express a falsehood too).

According to the attributer contextualist, then, the radical sceptical argument seems compelling precisely because there is something about the context in which we consider the sceptical problem that raises the epistemic standards and thereby ensures that the radical sceptic's conclusion that we don't know very much expresses a truth. But that is meant to be perfectly compatible with the fact that, relative to normal contexts where lower epistemic standings apply, we do count as having much of the knowledge that we take ourselves to have, including (given the closure principle) knowledge of the denials of sceptical hypotheses (more precisely, in these contexts assertions which ascribe knowledge to us tend to come out as true).

There are a few things to note about this proposal. First, notice why the view is called *attributer* contextualism. The reason for this is that it is the context of the one who is ascribing the knowledge that counts. So, for example, suppose that I am in a normal context where normal epistemic standards apply. Now imagine two people in different contexts evaluating my epistemic position as regards a certain proposition (e.g., that I have two hands). The first person is in a sceptical context where very demanding epistemic standards apply, whereas the second person is in a normal context where very undemanding epistemic standards apply (albeit a different normal context from the one that I am in). For both of these people what counts when they make their assessment of my epistemic position is not the epistemic standards in operation in *my* context, but rather the epistemic standards in operation in *their* respective contexts. Thus, the first person might assert 'Duncan doesn't know that he has two hands' and thereby express a truth, while the second person might assert 'Duncan does know that he has two hands' and thereby also express a truth. There is no contradiction here – it is not as if the one person is truly asserting '*p*' and the second person is truly asserting 'not-*p*' – since 'knows' on this view is a context-sensitive term which is picking out a different epistemic property when uttered by each of these speakers. (A useful comparison here is indexicals. When I say 'I am hungry' and you reply by saying 'I am not hungry', we are not contradicting each other even though it may superficially look as if our assertions are in opposition. This is because 'I' picks out a different person in each case.)

The second point we need to note is what the mechanism is that raises the epistemic standards. Why, for example, should talking about a radical sceptical hypothesis make the epistemic standards in play more demanding? There are various proposals in this respect. One popular suggestion is that in talking about an error possibility you thereby make it relevant, even if it would not have been relevant had you not mentioned it. So, for example, in normal contexts we don't consider sceptical hypotheses and other far-fetched error possibilities and hence the epistemic standards are low. Given that they are far-fetched error possibilities, there is nothing wrong with us failing to take them into account in this context. As soon as we start to consider them, however, then we do need to take them into account, and hence in order to qualify as having knowledge we now need to be able to rule out these error possibilities. But that's very hard to do; indeed, in the case of sceptical hypotheses it is, it seems, impossible to do. Thus, while it is very easy to possess knowledge in normal contexts, it is very hard to possess knowledge in sceptical contexts in which sceptical hypotheses are at issue.

There are a number of objections that have been levelled against attributer contextualism, but I want to focus here on three problems that I think are particularly pressing for the view. The first problem is what we might call the *problem of epistemic descent*. The worry here is that while attributer contextualism offers a fairly good explanation of how epistemic standards can get raised such that one no longer counts as having knowledge relative to the new epistemic standards, it isn't clear what kind of story it could possibly offer to explain how the epistemic standards would subsequently become lowered so that one would then count as having knowledge again. That is, if becoming aware of sceptical hypotheses suffices to raise the standards and thereby ensure that you no longer count as having knowledge, then how can it be that one can ever return to the state of innocence prior to one becoming aware of these hypotheses, and so be reunited with one's erstwhile knowledge? If the attributer contextualist cannot tell a good story about how epistemic descent works, then it seems that the most this proposal can offer is a good explanation of why other people who have never considered the sceptical hypotheses have the knowledge that they think they have; it cannot explain why we epistemologists, who have considered sceptical hypotheses, could have the knowledge that we think we have since, *qua* epistemologists, we would be forever unable to occupy a normal context in which undemanding epistemic standards are in operation.

The second problem for attributer contextualism is what we might call the *irrelevance of epistemic standards*. What is essential to the attributer contextualist response to radical scepticism is the idea that, relative to undemanding epistemic standards, we are in a position to know both everyday propositions (such as that we have hands) and also, given the closure principle, the denials of sceptical hypotheses, such as the BIV sceptical hypothesis. The problem is, however, that if the radical sceptical argument is correct, then it seems that we lack knowledge of these propositions relative to *any* epistemic standard, and thus making appeal to low epistemic standards is beside the point. After all, the radical sceptical claim is that we have no reason at all for thinking that we are not, say, BIVs and hence (given the closure principle) that we have no reason at all for thinking that we have hands – something that is incompatible with being a BIV. Thus if the radical sceptic is right, then we lack knowledge even relative to low epistemic standards, and hence the attributer contextualist's appeal to low epistemic standards is entirely irrelevant.

Perhaps the attributer contextualist can respond to these two worries – i.e., offer an adequate story as regards epistemic descent and also explain how we can have an epistemic standing as regards our beliefs such that they at least satisfy low epistemic standards. Even so, it would still face a third problem which concerns the dialectical effectiveness of this anti-sceptical proposal given an alternative anti-sceptical proposal that is available. We will call this the *problem of overkill*, for reasons that will soon become apparent.

To begin with, note that the premise in the sceptical argument that the attributer contextualist rejects is the first premise that we are unable to know the denials of sceptical hypotheses. Given that the attributer contextualist wishes to retain the closure principle, she has to reject this premise, since knowledge of everyday propositions will generate, via this principle, knowledge of the denials of sceptical hypotheses. The worry, however, is that if we can explain why this premise is false – i.e., if we can offer an epistemological story on which this premise no longer holds – then why should we offer in addition a contextualist account of 'knows'? After all, the mere fact that this premise is false will suffice to block the sceptical argument, and hence anything else is strictly speaking inessential to one's anti-sceptical position.

Of course, the attributer contextualist will respond to this by arguing that it is only in light of the attributer contextualist account of 'knows' that it makes sense to deny this premise, but the worry in play here is that, once we satisfy ourselves that it is possible to reject this premise, it ought to start to become plausible to think that this premise comes out as false relative to *any* context. Ultimately, the issue here is dialectical, since it rests on whether there is an alternative proposal available which merely denies this premise and which does not in addition endorse a contextualist account of 'knows'. The crux of the matter is that if there is a viable proposal in this regard, then it is at a considerable dialectical advantage relative to attributer contextualism since whereas attributer contextualism denies this premise and offers a contextualist account of 'knows', the alternative position merely denies this premise. As we will now see, there is a plausible proposal available in this regard, and hence attributer contextualism is faced with a stiff challenge on this front.

Responding to the closure-based sceptical argument III: neo-Mooreanism

This anti-sceptical proposal is known as *neo-Mooreanism*. Essentially, neo-Mooreanism argues that the first premise in the closure-based radical sceptical argument is false, and thus that we can know the denials of sceptical hypotheses. Crucially, however, this view is in no way allied to a contextualist account of 'knows'. In order to understand this view, we first need to understand why it is a 'neo'-Moorean position, and this means considering what a 'Moorean' anti-sceptical position would involve.

In a series of influential articles, G. E. Moore argued for what he regarded as being a very straightforward response to the problem of radical scepticism. Although the details of Moore's approach to radical scepticism are in fact quite subtle, we can delineate certain features that are held to be characteristic of a 'Moorean' response to the sceptical problem. The first is a common-sense conviction that we do know the denials of sceptical hypotheses and, what is more, that we know them on the basis of our knowledge of everyday propositions. So, for example, a Moorean might argue that since he knows full well that he has hands, he is also in a position to know that he is not a (handless) BIV. The second element is that the Moorean holds that it is perfectly reasonable to assert this knowledge, even in a context in which the sceptical problem is explicitly at issue. The third is that the Moorean holds that it is not required to offer an epistemological theory to explain how this anti-sceptical knowledge is possible, since that would only be required if the sceptic had raised a genuine problem regarding our knowledge, and by Moorean lights she hasn't.

It's actually unclear whether Moore himself would be willing to assent to each of these claims, at least as they are currently expressed at any rate, but in any case these claims are closely associated with his approach to scepticism ('Mooreanism' may thus be a position that Moore himself wouldn't endorse). Still, when philosophers talk of a 'Moorean' response to scepticism this is what they have in mind. Mooreanism is usually held to be a rather unattractive way of responding to the problem of radical scepticism, in that it seems to fail to engage with what the problem is really about. After all, to be told that common sense dictates that we must know the denials of sceptical hypotheses is hardly any help if we can't see how such knowledge could be possessed. Moreover, if we do have such knowledge, why does it seem so inappropriate to respond to the sceptic by arguing that one has it?

This is where neo-Mooreanism comes in. What is common between Mooreanism and neo-Mooreanism is that they both hold that one can know the denials of sceptical hypotheses, but here is where the similarities end. In particular, the neo-Mooreanism maintains that it is essential to tell an appropriate epistemological story about how such knowledge is possible, and also concedes that there is something 'fishy' about making 'Moorean' anti-sceptical assertions – e.g., asserting, in light of the sceptical problem, that one does know that one is not a BIV. Let us take these points in turn.

The epistemological story that the neo-Moorean standardly tells is an externalist one (though note that we will consider an internalist variant in a moment). According to this line, although it is true that one lacks good reflectively accessible grounds for believing that one is not the victim of a sceptical hypothesis, this fact alone should not decide the issue of whether one has knowledge of these propositions. In particular, the neo-Moorean typically argues that our beliefs in this regard satisfy certain externalist epistemic *desiderata*.

Consider, for example, whether one's belief in the denial of a sceptical hypothesis is *safe* – i.e., whether it is true not only in the actual world but also in all (or nearly all) nearby possible worlds as well. The first thing to note on this score is that if we do have the widespread knowledge that we credit to ourselves – such that the actual world is pretty much as we take it to be – then this would almost certainly entail that sceptical possible worlds are far-off worlds. But if that is the case, then our beliefs in the denials of sceptical hypotheses are safe by default, since clearly there cannot then be a near-by possible world where one continues to believe in the target proposition and yet that belief is false.

Indeed, it may be that our beliefs in the denials of sceptical hypotheses are inevitably safe even if there are near-by possible worlds where the sceptical hypothesis obtains. Recall that we noted above that, provided one relativizes the sensitivity principle to one's actual belief-forming method properly, then one's belief that one is not the victim of a sceptical hypothesis will be sensitive after all, despite first appearances. The reason for this is that in the nearest possible worlds where what one actually believes is no longer true – i.e., the worlds in which the target sceptical hypothesis obtains – although one will form a false belief in the target proposition, one won't form a false belief in this proposition *on the same basis* as in the actual world (since one's actual belief-forming method is by definition unavailable in a sceptical possible world). This point about methods applies with equal force to the safety principle, since we should in the same way relativize this principle to the actual belief-forming method used. But if that's right, then it follows that even if there is a sceptical possible world in the modal neighbourhood it won't be relevant to our assessment of whether the agent's belief in the denial of the target sceptical hypothesis is safe. Hence, that our agent would form a false belief that she is not the victim of this sceptical hypothesis in this world is entirely by the by, since this belief isn't formed on the same basis as in the actual world.

In any case, what seems to be true is that our beliefs in the denials of sceptical hypotheses are inevitably safe. But if one holds that the safety principle captures our intuition that knowledge must not be subject to epistemic luck (an issue we explored at length in chapter 2), then one will thus hold that there is something very significant speaking in favour of one's beliefs in the denials of sceptical hypotheses, epistemically speaking – *viz.*, that they are true beliefs that are immune to epistemic luck. The sceptical claim that knowledge of such propositions is impossible is thus starting to look far less secure.

The second element of the neo-Moorean position is the diagnostic story regarding why we are so tempted to think that we lack knowledge of the denials of sceptical hypotheses. For the externalist neo-Moorean, part of the story here will be to blame epistemic internalism. That is, the externalist will argue that it is epistemically internalist intuitions that are motivating the idea that knowledge of this sort is impossible. In contrast, or so the argument runs, once we move across to an 'enlightened' externalist epistemology we will see that our inability to offer good reflectively accessible grounds in favour of a belief is entirely compatible with our nonetheless having knowledge of the target proposition.

The externalist neo-Moorean can build on this point by arguing that it is our epistemic internalist intuitions which explain why to claim to know the denials of sceptical hypotheses also strikes us as inappropriate. The story here is complex, but the basic idea is that in claiming knowledge we represent ourselves as being able to offer appropriate supporting grounds in favour of what we claim to know. If that's right, however, then in cases where one's knowledge is not supported by reflectively accessible (and thus citable) supporting grounds, as in this case, the relevant assertion will be inappropriate even though it is true. That is, in claiming to know that, say, one is not a BIV, one is thereby representing oneself as being in possession of good and contextually appropriate reflectively accessible grounds in favour of the target proposition. And yet, intuitively at least, one inevitably lacks such grounds, since what could one offer by way of rational support in this regard? (That it seems to one as if one is not a BIV? But it seems to a BIV that she is not a BIV too.)

That a true assertion could be nonetheless inappropriate is not as odd as it might at first appear. Imagine, for example, the following case. Paul is asked where the nearest petrol station is and he replies that there is one just around the corner, even while knowing full well that this petrol station is presently closed. Strictly speaking, Paul spoke truly, since there is a petrol station around the corner, and yet his assertion was clearly inappropriate in that it implied that the petrol station in question was open, and this is false. Thus it is little wonder that we find this assertion improper. The neo-Moorean idea is that we can account for the impropriety of our claims to know the denials of radical sceptical hypotheses along the same lines. The trick is just to recognise that an assertion can be both true and yet improper, and that there are grounds for thinking that just such an eventuality obtains in this case.

Indeed, this point about the link between appropriate claims to know and the possession of reflectively accessible grounds can also go some way towards accommodating attributer contextualist intuitions within a neo-Moorean framework. After all, one could on this basis further argue that to claim to know even an everyday proposition can be inappropriate if one is in a context in which the sceptical problem is being actively considered. The idea in play here is that while ordinarily claiming such knowledge only implies that one can offer the normal kind of rational support for one's assertion, in contexts in which the sceptical problem is in play a different, and more austere, kind of rational support is required. For example, it could be that in a normal context one could legitimately claim to know that one's car is outside even while only having as supporting grounds that one saw it there earlier today. In a sceptical context, however, that very same assertion might be thought to imply that one has grounds sufficient for dismissing a relevant sceptical hypothesis – e.g., that one's car has not been stolen and replaced by a hologram. There is thus a kind of context-sensitivity in play here, but it is not as regards 'knows' but rather as regards the kind of reflectively accessible grounds that are needed in order to properly make a claim to know.

There is thus a lot to be said in favour of neo-Mooreanism, and since it avoids a commitment to a contextualist thesis about 'knows' it also has a dialectical advantage over attributer contextualism, as we noted above. Nevertheless, there are some fairly severe problems with the view. Perhaps the principal worry concerns the epistemological story regarding how we are able to know the denials of sceptical hypotheses. As we have argued earlier in this book, it does not suffice for knowledge that one has merely met an anti-luck condition; rather, one also needs to satisfy an ability condition. In particular – at least if the anti-luck virtue epistemology that we looked at in chapter 4 is correct – one's true belief needs to be the product of one's cognitive ability to the extent that one's safe cognitive success is to a significant degree creditable to one's cognitive agency. The trouble is, of course, that very little in the way of cognitive ability seems to be in play in this case. Rather, for the most part at least, one simply takes it for granted that the way the world appears to be is roughly how it is, and so long as one is generally correct in this regard, then one's belief ends up being safe. If this safe belief is not significantly creditable to one's cognitive ability, however, then it is hard to see why it would constitute knowledge.

One possible way round this might be to appeal to an internalist version of neo-Mooreanism. For example, one might appeal to a form of epistemological disjunctivism of the sort that we explored in chapter 5 and so argue on this basis that we do have good reflectively accessible grounds in favour of our beliefs in the denials of sceptical hypotheses. On this view, after all, provided that we are indeed in good cognitive conditions, our beliefs in everyday propositions will be supported by factive reflectively accessible grounds. If one has factive reflectively accessible support in favour of one's belief that, say, one has two hands, however, then it is hard to see how one could fail to have factive reflectively accessible support in favour of one's belief that one is not a BIV, at least if one is aware that BIVs don't have hands. Thus on this view there is far more speaking in favour of one's beliefs in the denials of sceptical hypotheses than simply that they are not subject to epistemic luck, since one in addition has good reflectively accessible rational support in favour of these beliefs.

Whatever the merits of this internalist rendering of the neo-Moorean thesis, it should be clear that it is subject to the same objection that was levelled at externalist neo-Mooreanism, since the point still remains that one can hardly regard one's belief that one is not a BIV as being due in the relevant way to the exercise of one's cognitive ability, no matter what its epistemic pedigree might otherwise be. It is not as if, for example, one possesses any kind of relevant discriminative capacity which was operative in this case, such as an ability to determine whether one is being deceived in this way. But if the cognitive ability in question is not a matter of possessing such a discriminative capacity, then in virtue of what is this belief due in the required way to one's cognitive ability?

Moreover, as things stand internalist neo-Mooreanism is unable to take advantage of the diagnostic story that externalist neo-Mooreanism offers to explain why we find it so intuitive to suppose that we can't know the denials of sceptical hypotheses. After all, on this view, we have a high degree of internalist epistemic support in favour of our beliefs in the denials of sceptical hypotheses. So why then are we so reluctant to regard ourselves as having knowledge in this respect? Furthermore, given that we have this high degree of internalist epistemic support for these beliefs, what is standing in the way of our properly claiming to have this knowledge (in any context)? It is thus vital that the internalist neo-Moorean is able to adduce her own diagnostic story in this regard.

Concluding remarks

There is thus no easy response available to the radical sceptical problem. Perhaps, however, we should not expect there to be. After all, as noted at the start of this chapter, the radical sceptical problem is, properly construed, a paradox, and hence it exposes a deep tension in our own concepts. With that in mind, it could well be that what we should settle for here is the anti-sceptical response that does the most justice to our intuitions while offering a resolution, albeit a partly counterintuitive resolution, to the problem. With this point in mind, all three of the anti-sceptical responses argued for here, despite their manifest problems, still have some scope for development.

Chapter summary

In this chapter we have examined the case for *radical scepticism*. As we saw, we can think of this problem as a putative *paradox* that attempts to expose a deep tension in our epistemological concepts. The version of the problem that we focussed on made essential appeal to both *radical sceptical hypotheses* and the *closure principle*. One response to the sceptical problem, so formulated, is to appeal to the *sensitivity principle* in order to motivate the idea that we should reject the closure principle. Once we take into account that the sensitivity principle is meant to be relativized to a particular belief-forming method, however, this motivation for denying the closure principle begins to look suspect. A second response to the sceptical problem involves appealing to *attributer contextualism*, which is the view that 'knows' is a context-sensitive term. On this proposal it can consistently be the case both that ascriptions of knowledge in everyday contexts express truths, and that corresponding ascriptions of knowledge in contexts in which the problem of radical scepticism is at issue express falsehoods. Finally, we looked at a third response to the problem, known as *neo-Mooreanism*. On this view one can know the denials of radical sceptical hypotheses. Usually this proposal is motivated by appeal to epistemic externalism, though we also saw that one can conceive of a version of the thesis that runs along epistemic internalist lines.

Further introductory reading

See Pritchard (2013, part four) for a very accessible overview of the contemporary debate as regards radical scepticism. See also Pritchard (2002a). See Pritchard (2010b) for a detailed annotated bibliography of the main literature on radical scepticism. See also Pritchard (2002c) and Klein (2015), listed below under 'free internet resources'.

Further advanced reading

For a key recent discussion of the closure principle, see the exchange between Dretske (2014a; 2014b) and Hawthorne (2014). The key defence of infallibilism can be found in Unger (1975). The two key rejections of the closure principle can be found in Dretske (1970) and Nozick (1981). An important critique of the denial of the closure principle can be found in Stine (1976). For further defence of the claim that the sensitivity principle, properly understood, does not generate the counterexamples to the closure principle that it advertises, see M. Williams (1991, ch. 9) and Black (2002). For the key defences of attributer contextualism as a response to scepticism, see DeRose (1995), Lewis (1996) and Cohen (2000). For a useful survey of work on contextualism, see Rysiew (2011). For two central defences of a different kind of contextualism, one that focuses on the subject's context rather than the attributer's context, see Hawthorne (2004) and Stanley (2005). For two useful introductions to contextualism in epistemology, see Black (2003) and Rysiew (2007). For Moore's main writings on scepticism, see Moore (1925; 1939; 1959). For some of the central defences of neo-Mooreanism, see Sosa (1999) and Pritchard (2002b; 2005; 2007b; 2008b). For a defence of a specifically internalist neo-Mooreanism, see Pritchard (2012b). See also Pritchard (2015b; cf. Pritchard 2015 *forthcoming a*), which combines this proposal with Wittgensteinian insights about the problem of radical scepticism. For more on the point that true assertions can nonetheless be inappropriate, see Grice (1989).

Free internet resources
See Pritchard (2002c) and Klein (2015) for two helpful overviews of the contemporary debate regarding radical scepticism.

Study questions
1. What is the difference between conceiving of the problem of radical scepticism as a *paradox* as opposed to a *position*?
2. What is a radical sceptical hypothesis, and why might one hold that one can never know the denials of radical sceptical hypotheses? Try to formulate your own radical sceptical hypothesis.
3. What is the closure principle? Do you find this principle plausible?
4. How does radical scepticism employ the closure principle? Why can't radical scepticism simply appeal to the fact that we are unable to know the denials of radical sceptical hypotheses?
5. Why might one hold that if sensitivity is a requirement on knowledge, then we should deny the closure principle? Is this a good basis for denying the closure principle, do you think?
6. What is attributer contextualism? How plausible is this proposal as a response to radical scepticism?
7. What is neo-Mooreanism, and how does it differ from Mooreanism?
8. How might one combine neo-Mooreanism with epistemic internalism? Would such a view be more plausible than a version of neo-Mooreanism that is cast along epistemic externalist lines?

Sample essay questions
1. What role does the closure principle play in the radical sceptical paradox? Is denying such a principle a possible way of resolving the paradox?
2. Critically evaluate responses to the problem of radical scepticism that maintain that one can know the denials of radical sceptical hypotheses. Are any of these anti-sceptical proposals plausible?
3. What is the attributer contextualist response to the problem of radical scepticism? How effective is this treatment of the radical scepticism problem?

7
Epistemic Value

The value problem for knowledge

It is widely held that knowledge is of distinctive value. Presumably, this is the reason why knowledge – and not, say, justified true belief – has been the principal focus of generations of epistemological theorising. Understanding just why knowledge is distinctively valuable, however, has proved elusive and this has led some to question whether it is distinctively valuable at all. Call this the *value problem*.

Part of the difficulty posed by the value problem involves getting clear about just what it means to say that knowledge is distinctively valuable. One minimal reading of this claim is that knowledge is more valuable than mere true belief. Call the challenge to explain why knowledge is more valuable than mere true belief the *primary value problem*. Clearly there is more to showing that knowledge is distinctively valuable than answering this problem, and we will consider what additional demands a response to the value problem needs to satisfy in a moment. What ought to be clear, however, is that if we are unable to account even for why knowledge is more valuable than mere true belief then the very project of answering the value problem is a lost cause.

On the face of it, there is a very straightforward answer to the primary value problem – *viz.*, that knowledge is more valuable than mere true belief because it tends to be of greater practical value. Of course, there may be particular propositions that, for some special reason, one would prefer to merely truly believe rather than know (perhaps in knowing them one would incur a penalty which one wouldn't incur if one merely true believed them), but in general you are more likely to achieve your goals with knowledge than with mere true belief.

Indeed, this is precisely the way that Socrates answers the primary value problem in Plato's dialogue, the *Meno*. Why should you prefer knowledge of the correct way to the city of Larissa rather than mere true belief, given that both will, on the face of it, ensure that you get to your destination? Socrates's answer is that knowledge has a 'stability' which mere true belief lacks. Mere true belief, argues Socrates, is like one of the untethered statues of Daedalus – statues so life-like that they were reputed to run away if not tied down – in that it is liable to be lost. Knowledge, in contrast, is like one of those statues tethered. For while a mere true belief may well enable you to achieve your goals as well as knowledge, one will be far more insulated from failure by possessing knowledge.

Suppose, for example, that the road to Larissa takes an unexpected course. Someone with mere true belief – where the belief is based on just a hunch, say – may well at this point lose all faith that she is on the right tracks and turn back. Someone who knows that this is the right way to go, however – perhaps because she consulted a reliable map before her departure – will not be so shaken by this turn of events.

At least generally speaking, then, we can say that knowledge is more valuable than mere true belief because it has a practical value which mere true belief lacks. In this way we can respond to at least the primary value problem.

The swamping problem

There is a very different problem about epistemic value that is often posed alongside the challenge that Socrates responds to in the *Meno*. This is known as the *swamping problem*. Although these two problems are superficially very similar, however, there is also a crucial difference. In order to understand this difference, we first need to notice an important ambiguity in the very notion of 'epistemic value'. Read one way, to say that something has epistemic value is to say that it has a value that is specifically epistemic. Read another way, when we talk about epistemic value we might instead have in mind the particular kinds of value that attach to epistemic standings. We can think of this latter usage of 'epistemic value' as being concerned with the *value of the epistemic*, rather than with epistemic value specifically. Notice that these two understandings of 'epistemic value' are not equivalent. After all, knowledge might be more valuable than mere true belief even while having no more specifically epistemic value than true belief. It is thus crucial to keep these two notions of epistemic value apart.

The response to the primary value problem that Socrates offers in the Meno does not appeal to a particular kind of epistemic value that knowledge has but which mere true belief lacks. Instead, he appeals to the greater practical value of knowledge over true belief, where this is not a specifically epistemic kind of value. In contrast, the swamping problem, as we will now see, is explicitly concerned with the question of whether knowledge is more valuable, from an exclusively epistemic point of view, than mere true belief. The problem raised by the swamping problem is that at least on a certain conception of what counts as epistemic value, it isn't at all obvious that knowledge could be epistemically better than mere true belief.

In order to get a handle on this problem, we need to consider an analogy that is often offered to motivate this difficulty. Imagine that one is presented with two cups of coffee that are identical in every respect: they taste the same, look the same, are the same quantity, and so on. Should it matter to you which cup you take? Presumably not. (If it helps, ask yourself the question whether you would be willing to pay more for one of these cups of coffee.) Here is the twist in the tale, however. Whereas one of the cups of coffee was produced by a coffee-making machine which regularly produces great coffee, the other cup of coffee was produced by a coffee-making machine which usually produces very poor coffee, though as it happened produced a great cup of coffee on this particular occasion. Here is the crux of the matter: it seems that the different ways that these cups of coffee were produced ought not to make any difference to how we value them – insofar as they are identical cups of coffee, we should value them the same. After all, we only care about whether a coffee-making machine is reliable at producing good coffee because we care about good coffee. So once we've actually got the good coffee in front of us, as we do on this occasion, then it shouldn't matter anymore how the coffee was produced.

The reason why this analogy is important is that we can run a similar argument for knowledge and mere true belief. Knowledge, after all, is true belief that is acquired in an epistemically good fashion. Mere true belief, in contrast, is presumably a belief which was acquired in an epistemically deficient fashion, but which happened to lead to lead to a true belief on this occasion. Why do we care about forming our beliefs in an epistemically good way? Well, presumably, this is because we recognise that gaining true beliefs is epistemically valuable. But if the coffee analogy is right, then it seems that from a purely epistemic point of view it shouldn't matter to us whether a belief is formed in an epistemically good fashion or not, so long as it is true. Rather, faced

Epistemic Value 115

with two true beliefs, only one of which amounts to knowledge, we should regard them as equally valuable from a specifically epistemic point of view, just as we regard the two cups of coffee described above as equally valuable.

The point is that if we only care about forming our beliefs in epistemically good ways because this is a means to true belief, then when we have the true belief in question the belief is not made any more valuable from an epistemic point of view by being formed in an epistemically good way. (Just as the great coffee isn't made any more valuable from a coffee point of view by being produced by a coffee-making machine that regularly produces great coffee.) As we might put the point, the value of the presence of the true belief (/great coffee) 'swamps' whatever value might be in play in virtue of the true belief (/great coffee) being formed in an epistemically good way (/being produced by a coffee-making machine which regularly produces great coffee).

Notice that in order for the swamping problem to go through, it is important that we have a conception of epistemic value such that the fundamental epistemic good is true belief. In particular, we need a conception of epistemic value such that we only epistemically value the kinds of belief-forming processes that generate positive epistemic standings like knowledge and justification because they are truth-conducive – i.e., because they generally lead to true beliefs. We can refer to such a conception of epistemic value as *epistemic value truth monism*. The view is a form of monism, because it insists that there is only one fundamental epistemic good. And since that sole fundamental epistemic good is true belief, so we get the idea that it is form of truth monism.

Epistemic value truth monism has historically been a popular way of thinking about epistemic value. After all, it does seem distinctive of the epistemic realm that it is directed towards truth. But if one rejects such a view then one might be able to motivate a response to the swamping problem. For example, one might endorse a form of *epistemic value pluralism*, whereby there is more than one fundamental epistemic good. Perhaps, for example, one holds that there are other fundamental epistemic goods besides truth? On such a view, it could be that knowledge is epistemically better than mere true belief because it has more of these other fundamental epistemic goods. Another possibility is a form of epistemic value monism where true belief is not the fundamental epistemic good. Suppose, for example, that one held that knowledge is the fundamental epistemic good: a view that we might call *epistemic value knowledge monism*. It would obviously follow that knowledge is of greater epistemic value than mere true belief.

Before we abandon epistemic value truth monism, however, we might want to consider whether the swamping problem is such a serious difficulty in the first place. After all, the swamping problem only says that knowledge is not epistemically more valuable than mere true belief, and as we noted above this claim is entirely compatible with the idea that knowledge is in general more valuable than mere true belief (e.g., that it might have more practical value, as Socrates contends). Is it really so counterintuitive that knowledge is not better from a purely epistemic point of view than mere true belief? More precisely, insofar as one is persuaded by epistemic value truth monism, it's not clear why one should be concerned by this conclusion. Rather than being a problem for the view, isn't it simply what the view amounts to?

In any case, in what follows we will set the swamping problem to one side and focus on the question of whether knowledge is in general of distinctive value, whether that value is specifically epistemic or otherwise.

Back to the value problem for knowledge

Let's grant that we can respond to the primary value problem by appealing to greater practical value of knowledge over mere true belief as Socrates maintains. Even so, however, there would still be more to do to secure our intuition that knowledge is distinctively valuable. At the very least, we would need to answer the *secondary value problem* of explaining why knowledge is more valuable than any proper subset of its parts.

In order to see this, suppose that one answered the primary value problem by, for example, pointing to a necessary condition for knowledge which in general added practical value (the justification condition, say), but suppose further that the satisfaction of this condition, in conjunction with true belief, was not sufficient for knowledge. Perhaps, for example, when one knows that p it is the fact that one's belief that p is thereby justified that ensures that knowledge has a greater practical value than mere true belief that p alone. One would thereby have answered the primary value problem while leaving the secondary value problem unanswered (because, as Gettier showed us, there is more to knowledge than just justified true belief). Moreover, let us take it as given that there is no further feature of knowledge that is value-conferring, such that the secondary value problem is regarded not just as unanswered, but as unanswerable.

On the face of it, this lacuna might not seem that problematic, since just so long as one can show that knowledge is more valuable than mere true belief then that would seem to satisfy our intuition that knowledge is of some special value to us (on this view it is, after all, the kind of thing that we should prefer to mere true belief, all other things being equal). The problem, however, is that if the distinctive value of knowledge is due to some feature of knowledge which, with true belief, falls short of knowledge, then it seems that what we should seek is not knowledge as such, but rather that which falls short of knowledge (i.e., true belief plus the value-conferring property X, in this case justification). But if that's right, then why do we regard knowledge as distinctively valuable at all?

The primary value problem thus naturally leads to the secondary value problem, and it seems that both will need to be answered if we are to account for the distinctive value of knowledge. Intuitively, however, there seems no in-principle reason why the 'practical' response to the primary value problem just noted could not be extended to the secondary value problem. That is, just as knowledge is of greater practical value than mere true belief, in that it is the kind of thing that better enables us to attain our goals, so knowledge is of greater practical value than any epistemic standing that falls short of knowledge for the same reason.

Even if we can offer a response to the secondary value problem, however, it is still not clear that we have accounted for the distinctive value of knowledge. This is because the secondary value problem leaves open the possibility that the difference of value at issue is merely one of degree rather than kind. To say that knowledge is of *distinctive* value, however, appears to suggest that the difference in value between knowledge and that which falls short of knowledge is not just a matter of degree, but of *kind*. After all, if one regards knowledge as being more valuable than that which falls short of knowledge merely as a matter of degree rather than kind, then this has the effect of putting knowledge on a kind of continuum of value, albeit further up the continuum than anything that falls short of knowledge. The problem with this 'continuum' account of the value of knowledge, however, is that it fails to explain why the long history of epistemological discussion has focussed specifically on the stage in this continuum of epistemic value that knowledge marks rather than some other stage (such as a stage just before the one marked out by knowledge, or just after). Accordingly, it seems that accounting for our intuitions about the value of knowledge requires us to offer an explanation of why knowledge has not just a greater *degree* but also a different *kind* of value than whatever falls short of knowledge. Call this the *tertiary value problem*.

Further support for the tertiary value problem comes from the fact that we often treat knowledge as being, unlike lesser epistemic standings, *precious*, in the sense that its value is not merely a function of its practical import. In this sense, knowledge is akin to, say, a beautiful painting or an historically important artefact, such as the first ever printing press. While both a beautiful painting and the first ever printing press are clearly valuable as a means to other things – they will have a monetary value, for example, and so can be sold in order to enable one to buy other items that one desires – we do not value them simply as a means to further ends but rather regard them as precious items which are valuable in their own right. That is, we regard them as having non-instrumental value, otherwise known as *final* value. If knowledge, unlike lesser epistemic standings, is indeed precious in this way, then it follows that it too must have a final value that lesser epistemic standings lack.

Most of those who have explored the issue of the value of knowledge have tended to focus their attentions on the primary value problem, to the exclusion of the other two problems. There is a good rationale for a focus of this sort, since if one is unable to answer the primary value problem then, *a fortiori*, one will be unable to answer the secondary and tertiary problems as well. This rationale can be turned on its head, however, since it equally follows that if one could offer a response to the tertiary value problem then one would thereby be able to deal with the primary and secondary value problems as well.

Knowledge, achievement and final value

Interestingly, there is a proposal in the literature which, if effective, would offer a very straightforward response to the tertiary value problem. Recall the robust virtue epistemic account of knowledge that we considered in chapter three:

Robust Virtue Epistemology
S knows that p if and only if S's belief that p is true because it was formed via the reliable cognitive traits that make up her cognitive character.

In essence, this proposal construes knowledge as a cognitive success (i.e., true belief) that is because of cognitive ability (i.e., primarily creditable to the exercise of one's cognitive ability). As we noted in chapter three, what is significant about this way of thinking about knowledge is that it appears to make knowledge into a kind of *achievement*. That is, we might broadly think of achievements as being successes that are because of one's ability (i.e., primarily creditable to the exercise of one's ability), and virtue epistemology seems to be offering the epistemic analogue of this claim – on this view, knowledge is cognitive success that is because of one's cognitive ability. As we will see, that knowledge turns out to be a type of achievement on this proposal is key to its defence of the final value of knowledge.

We noted in chapter three that the general account of achievements in play here is plausible. Mere success will not suffice for achievements if skill is not involved. But even when skill is involved, if there is not the right explanatory connection between success and skill – as when the success is Gettiered – then this won't lead to an achievement either. What is required is rather that one's success is because of one's abilities. Call this the *achievement* thesis.

There are some problems with the achievement thesis, which we will explore below. For now, however, we will let this claim stand. What is important for our current purposes is that if this account of achievement is right, then it follows that knowledge, by the lights of robust virtue epistemology at any rate, is just a specifically cognitive type of achievement. That is, achievements are successes that are because of ability and yet knowledge, according to robust virtue epistemology, is just cognitive success (i.e., true belief) that is because of cognitive ability (i.e., epistemic virtue, broadly conceived). The achievement thesis when combined with robust virtue epistemology thus entails the claim that knowledge is a type of achievement, what we will call the *knowledge-as-achievement* thesis, or the *K=A thesis* for short.

The reason why the K=A thesis is important for our purposes is because achievements are, plausibly, distinctively valuable. More specifically, it is plausible to hold that the kind of successes that count as achievements are valuable for their own sake because of how they are produced (i.e., they are finally valuable because of their relational properties). If this is right, and we can show that knowledge (unlike that which falls short of knowledge) is a type of achievement, then we may be in a position to thereby show that knowledge has a kind of value – final value – which that which falls short of knowledge lacks, and hence show that it is distinctively valuable.

In order to see why achievements are finally valuable, consider the case of an archer who – in the manner of Robin Hood – is trying to escape from an adversary and the target he is firing at is a mechanism which will drop the drawbridge in front him, thereby ensuring that he gets to safety. From a practical point of view, it may not matter whether the hitting of the target is because of the archer's archery abilities or through dumb luck (e.g., by a lucky deflection). Either way, it still results in the dropping of the drawbridge, thereby enabling our hero to escape. Nevertheless, wouldn't we value this success very differently if it were the product of luck (even when the relevant ability is involved, but the success in question is 'Gettierized'), rather than it being because of his ability such that it is an achievement? In particular, it seems that we would regard the archer's achievement of hitting the target through ability as, in this respect, a good thing in its own right, regardless of what other instrumental value it may accrue.

Moreover, what goes here for the archer's achievement of hitting the target seems to be equally applicable to achievements more generally: achievements are finally valuable. Imagine, for example, that you are about to undertake a course of action designed to attain a certain outcome and that you are given the choice between merely being successful in what you set out to do, and being successful in such a way that you exhibit an achievement. Suppose further that it is stipulated in advance that there are no practical costs or benefits to choosing either way. Even so, wouldn't you prefer to exhibit an achievement? And wouldn't you be right to do so? If that's correct, then this is strong evidence for the final value of achievements.

Indeed, that achievements are valuable in this way is hardly surprising once one reflects that they constitute the exercise of one's agency on the world. A life lacking in such agential power, even if otherwise successful (e.g., one's goals are regularly attained), would clearly be severely impoverished as a result. A good life is thus, amongst other things, a life rich in achievement. Call the claim that achievements are finally valuable the *value of achievements* thesis.

Now, if knowledge is simply a type of achievement, and achievements are finally valuable, then it immediately follows that knowledge has final value too. Robust virtue epistemology, when combined with a claim about the nature of achievements (the achievement thesis) and a claim about the final value of achievements (the value of achievements thesis), thus entails the thesis that knowledge has final value. More formally, we can express the reasoning in play here as follows:

From Robust Virtue Epistemology to the Final Value of Knowledge
(P1) Achievements are successes that are because of ability. (Achievement Thesis)

(P2) Knowledge is a cognitive success that is because of cognitive ability. (Robust Virtue Epistemology)
(C1) So, knowledge = cognitive achievement. (K=A Thesis)
(P3) Achievements are finally valuable. (Value of Achievements Thesis)
(C2) So, knowledge has final value.

Since the inferences in play here are clearly valid, if one wishes to object to this argument then one will need to deny one of the premises in play. In fact, there are problems with all three premises.

First off, consider (P1), the achievement thesis. A key difficulty facing this claim is that on this view even very easy successes that are the product of ability, such as raising one's arm, would count as an achievement. Normally, however, we don't count such easy successes as achievements at all. More precisely, it is part of our intuitive notion of an achievement that it either involves great skill or the overcoming of a significant obstacle. For example, if one is recovering from a major operation, then raising one's arm could well count as an achievement, since this would be a very hard thing to do in those circumstances. Alternatively, some 'easy' successes do count as achievements, but only because of the great skill involved. That a highly skilled tennis player can hit a difficult shot with ease does not undermine the achievement since great skill is being displayed.

Notice that it is not possible for the defender of (P1) to tighten up her conception of achievements in order to accommodate these points, since if she does then many cognitive successes will no longer count as achievements and hence the import of the view to epistemology will be lost. After all, lots of our cognitive successes – such as the beliefs formed when one opens one's eyes in the morning – are easy and do not involve the exercise of great cognitive skill. Nonetheless, they do count as knowledge.

Instead, then, perhaps the defender of (P1) could respond to this objection in a different way by arguing that they are defending a very broad conception of achievement, one that merely involves success that is because of ability. We would thus have two versions of the achievement thesis in play: a weak (inclusive) version which is the thesis that the robust virtue epistemologist has in mind, and a strong (restrictive) version more closely tied to our intuitive thinking about achievement which demands that the success in question involve either great skill or the overcoming of a significant obstacle. Now it is perfectly open to robust virtue epistemologists to offer an alternative conception of achievements in this way. The crux of the matter, however, will be whether this weaker version of the achievement thesis will still serve their purposes.

I think it is clear that it will not, since with the achievement thesis so construed it now ceases to even less plausible that (P3), the value of achievements thesis, is true. Even on the strong conception of achievements one might legitimately doubt this claim, since it would treat even wicked or pointless successes as potential achievements and thus as being of final value, and yet we typically do not think that successes of this sort are valuable in this way. Still, that even wicked or trivial achievements which involve great skill or the overcoming of a significant obstacle have some final value – perhaps of merely a *pro tanto* kind – is at least a *prima facie* plausible claim. Once one moves to the weak achievement thesis, however, then the problem becomes even more severe, since now even very easy successes, like raising one's arm, can count as achievements and hence be deserving of final value, and yet this is wildly unintuitive.

Even if the proponent of robust virtue epistemology can avoid these problems that confront premises (P1) and (P3), it would still face the problems raised for the view in chapter three. Recall that we argued there that there are cases of knowledge that do not fit with the robust virtue epistemic rubric. In particular, there are cases of knowledge where the agent's true belief is not because of her cognitive ability, and there are cases of true belief that are because of the agent's cognitive ability which don't constitute knowledge. (P2), the robust virtue epistemic claim that knowledge is cognitive success that is because of cognitive ability, is therefore highly questionable. Relatedly, if the robust virtue epistemologist is right that we should think of achievements as cognitive successes that are because of cognitive ability, then it follows that there are cases of knowledge that are not cases of cognitive achievement, and cases of cognitive achievement which are not cases of knowledge. The K=A thesis is therefore unsustainable.

The upshot of the foregoing is that the case offered by robust virtue epistemology for the final value of knowledge is not very compelling on closer inspection. Indeed, just about every moving part in that argument seems questionable. This doesn't mean that there isn't a viable solution to the tertiary value problem, of course, but it does suggest that the solution to this problem is unlikely to be found in this quarter. Alternatively, we could take the failure of the robust virtue epistemic response to the tertiary value problem to be an indication that perhaps knowledge isn't distinctively valuable as we have hitherto supposed. This is precisely the possibility that will be taken up in the next chapter.

Chapter summary

In this chapter we have encountered the *value problem for knowledge*. In its most immediate form – known as the *primary value problem* – this is the challenge of explaining why knowledge is more valuable than mere true belief. We saw that one historically influential response to this problem – offered by Socrates in Plato's dialogue the *Meno* – is that knowledge is more valuable than mere true belief because it has a greater degree of practical value. We contrasted this way of thinking about the primary value problem with a distinct difficulty regarding epistemic value known as the *swamping problem*. As we saw, while the primary value problem merely asks why knowledge is more valuable than mere true belief, the swamping problem is specifically concerned with why knowledge has a greater degree of epistemic value – i.e., value from a purely epistemic point of view – than mere true belief. The swamping problem turns on a particular conception of epistemic value known as *epistemic value truth monism*. One route out of the problem is thus to replace this account of epistemic value with a different proposal, either one which is pluralistic about epistemic value, or which offers a different kind of monism. Another possibility is to argue that proponents of epistemic value truth monism have nothing to fear from the swamping problem, in that the conclusion of that argument ought not to be thought counterintuitive to someone who proposes such a view. The primary value problem was then distinguished from the *secondary value problem* and the *tertiary value problem*. The former is the challenge of explaining why knowledge is more valuable than that which falls short of knowledge. The latter is the challenge of explaining why knowledge is more valuable than that which falls short of knowledge as a matter of kind rather than degree. As we saw, the motivation for the tertiary value problem is the idea that knowledge marks a distinctively valuable kind of epistemic standing, whereby knowledge, unlike epistemic standings which fall short of knowledge (such as justified true belief), is valuable in its own right (i.e., *finally valuable*). We considered one influential contemporary response to the tertiary value problem, offered by robust virtue epistemology. According to this proposal, knowledge is a kind of achievement. But since achievements are plausibly finally valuable, so we can in this way defend the final value of knowledge. This proposal faces a number of difficulties, however, not least because robust virtue epistemology is itself a questionable theory of knowledge.

Further introductory reading

For a very accessible introduction to the primary value problem, and the response to that problem offered by Socrates in Plato's dialogue the *Meno*, see Pritchard (2013, ch. 2). For a general survey of work on the value of knowledge, see Pritchard (2007c) and Greco (2011). See also Pritchard & Turri (2014), which is also listed below under free internet resources. For an annotated bibliography of recent work on the value of knowledge, see Olsson (2013). For an accessible account of the nature and value of achievements, see Pritchard (2010a).

Further advanced reading

The key discussion of the value of knowledge in the contemporary literature is Kvanvig (2003). The most explicit defence of the final value of knowledge along robust virtue-theoretic lines can be found in Greco (2009a). See also Greco (2009b). For an in-depth discussion of the some of the issues raised in this chapter, see Pritchard, Millar & Haddock (2010, chs. 1–4). For an exploration of how the debate regarding the value of knowledge can have an impact on our understanding of the problem of radical scepticism, see Pritchard (2008b).

Free internet resources

For a recent comprehensive survey of work on the value of knowledge, see Pritchard & Turri (2014).

Study questions

1. What is the primary value problem? How does Socrates answer that problem in Plato's dialogue the *Meno*? Do you find this proposal convincing?
2. What is epistemic value, specifically, and how does it differ from the value of the epistemic? Is Socrates appealing to a distinctively epistemic kind of value in his response to the primary value problem, or is he appealing instead to a non-epistemic kind of value?
3. What is the swamping problem? How does the analogy with coffee motivate this problem?
4. What is epistemic value truth monism, and how is it challenged by the swamping problem?
5. Are there any plausible alternatives to epistemic value truth monism?
6. What is the secondary value problem, and how does it differ from the primary value problem?

7. What is the tertiary value problem, and how does it differ from the secondary value problem? Relatedly, what is final value?
8. What is robust virtue epistemology, and why does such a proposal suggest that knowledge might be a particular kind of achievement?
9. How might robust virtue epistemology be able to appeal to the notion of achievements in order to answer the tertiary value problem?
10. Are achievements in general finally valuable? Does it matter how the notion of an achievement is understood?

Sample essay questions
1. 'Knowledge is more valuable than mere true belief'. Discuss.
2. What is the swamping problem? Does this problem demonstrate that epistemic value truth monism is unsustainable?
3. How might the proponent of robust virtue epistemology defend the final value of knowledge? Is such a proposal plausible?

8
Understanding

Introductory remarks

The failure of the robust virtue epistemic defence of the final value of knowledge should make us reconsider the intuition that knowledge is precious. Are we right to value knowledge in this way? I'm inclined to think that reflecting on the value problem ultimately reveals to us that the answer to this question is 'no'. Knowledge may be of great practical value – and if so its great practical value will give us a way of responding to the primary and secondary value problems – but it is not the kind of thing which is in its nature precious in the way that, say, a beautiful painting is. (Note that this is not to deny that *some* knowledge may be precious in this way.)

Does that mean that there is no distinctively valuable epistemic standing? I suggest not. In particular, there does seem to be a kind of epistemic standing which is in its nature a kind of achievement, and which would inherit the final value of achievements of this sort. This epistemic standing is *understanding*.

The intuition that understanding is distinctively valuable is surely even stronger than the intuition that knowledge is distinctively valuable. Indeed, insofar as knowledge and understanding come apart – I will be defending that the claim that they do in a moment – then understanding seems to be preferable to knowledge. As we might be tempted to put the point, we would surely rather understand than merely know. If that is right, and assuming that knowledge and understanding do come apart, then it would be premature to conclude from the fact that knowledge is, on closer inspection, not distinctively valuable that therefore neither is understanding. Instead, we should treat these two issues as potentially separate from one another. Before we can evaluate a claim of this sort, however, we need to be a little clearer about what we are talking about.

Understanding and knowledge

One problem that afflicts any direct comparison between knowledge and understanding is that knowledge (of the propositional sort that we have been focussing on at any rate) is concerned with propositions, whereas understanding usually isn't, at least not directly anyway. That is, the kind of knowledge we are interested in is knowledge that p, but it is rare to talk of understanding that p.

I want to take the paradigm usage of 'understands' to be in a statement like 'I understand why such-and-such is the case', as when a scientist might say that she understands why certain chemical reaction occurred. Call this type of understanding, *causal understanding*. Notice that this usage is very different from a more holistic usage which applies to subject matters, as in 'I understand quantum physics', or even 'I understand my partner'. I think the holistic usage of 'understands' is related to the non-holistic, or atomistic, usage that is our focus, but the former raises problems of its own that we've not the space to cover here (though we will flag some of these problems as we go along).

The standard view about causal understanding, at least in the philosophy of science literature, is that it is basically just (propositional) knowledge of causes. Imagine that I come home from work to find that my house has burned down. Consider what would be involved in my gaining an understanding of why my house has burned down – i.e., an understanding of what has caused this event to happen. Let us stipulate that the cause of the house burning down is faulty wiring. On the standard view of causal understanding, to understand why one's house burned down is to *know why* one's house burned down, which is turn is just to *know that* one's house burned down because of (in this case) faulty wiring. There is thus a straightforward sense in which causal understanding is just a variety of propositional knowledge that is concerned with knowledge of the cause of the event in question.

The standard view is broadly correct, though as we will see below, it might require some modification. But our interest just now is not in these subtleties but rather in the broad features of causal understanding. (Note: Henceforth, when I talk of understanding without qualification it will be causal understanding that I have in mind.) The first point to note, which I think many find initially surprising, is that understanding, just like knowledge, is *factive*. That is, I cannot understand why my house burned down if I have a false belief regarding why this event took place. Suppose, for example, that I believe that my house burned down because of faulty wiring, but that this is false. Surely, then, I would have no understanding of why my house burned down regardless of how strong my justification is for believing this proposition, or how well this belief coheres with the rest of the things I believe that are relevant in this respect (e.g., my beliefs about how faulty wiring can cause house fires). For sure, I *thought* I understood – indeed, it could well be that I *reasonably* (or at least *blamelessly*) thought that I understood – but the fact remains that I did not understand. In this respect, then, understanding is a lot like knowledge.

Part of the reason why many may find this claim initially surprising is because when it comes to the more holistic conception of understanding it *is* plausible to suppose that one's understanding is compatible with at least *some* false beliefs about the relevant subject matter. For example, I can surely have some false beliefs about quantum physics and yet be truly said to understand quantum physics. Even here, however, I think it is clear that the error involved had better be minor and relatively peripheral if one is to be properly accorded understanding. If one's beliefs about quantum physics are fundamentally awry, for example, then one simply does not understand quantum physics. In any case, this is all by the by, since the type of understanding we are concerned with here is not of this holistic sort.

One key difference between knowledge and understanding, at least on certain conceptions of knowledge at any rate, is that understanding is of its nature an epistemically internalist notion. That is, it is hard to make sense of how an agent could possess understanding and yet lack good reflectively accessible grounds in support of that understanding. Imagine, for example, someone understanding why his house burned down but, when asked why it burned down, was unable to offer an explanation of this event. Clearly here we would not regard this agent as having understanding, even if his beliefs in this respect were true and formed in externalistically respectable ways (e.g., via a reliable process). Understanding thus cannot be 'opaque' to the subject in the way that knowledge, by externalist lights at least, can sometimes be.

This difference between understanding and (an externalist treatment of) knowledge has led some commentators to argue that understanding also has a different relationship to epistemic luck than knowledge, in the sense that understanding is more compatible with epistemic luck than knowledge is. That is, the claim is that just as one's justification, internalistically conceived, is not undermined by epistemic luck (just the sufficiency of that justification, with true belief, for knowledge), so one's understanding is not undermined either. I think there is some truth in this claim, though as it stands it is not quite right.

Consider again the example of understanding why one's house burned down. Suppose first that we have a standard Gettier-style case in which something 'intervenes' between the agent's belief and the target fact, on the model of the Roddy case considered in chapter 1, in order to ensure that one's true belief is only true as a matter of luck, and so is unsafe. (Recall that we referred to this kind of epistemic luck as *intervening epistemic luck* in chapter 3). Here is a suitable scenario:

> *Alexander*
> Alexander comes home to find his house in flames. He approaches someone who looks as if she is the fire officer in charge and asks her what the reason for the fire is. He is told by this person that the reason why his house is burning down is faulty wiring, and this coheres with his wider set of beliefs (e.g., about how faulty wiring can cause a house fire). The person Alexander is speaking to, however, is not in fact a fire officer at all but instead someone who is merely dressed in a fire officer's uniform and who is on her way to a fancy dress party. Even so, what she said to Alexander was true: faulty wiring *was* the cause of this fire.

Clearly, the epistemic luck in play here prevents Alexander from having knowledge of why his house has burned down (i.e., he does not know that his house burnt down because of faulty wiring). The question in hand for us, however, is whether he likewise lacks understanding in this case. Seemingly, he does, since intuitively one cannot gain an understanding of why one's house burnt down by consulting someone who is not the fire officer but rather someone in fancy dress who is merely guessing the cause of the fire.

So does this mean that understanding is incompatible with epistemic luck in the way that knowledge is after all? Not entirely, since there is a different kind of epistemic luck – what we referred to as *environmental epistemic luck* in chapter 3, and which we noted was found in the Barney case first introduced in chapter 1 – which is knowledge-undermining but which does seem to be compatible with understanding. In cases of environmental epistemic luck the luckiness of one's true belief is entirely due to the fact that one is in an epistemically unfriendly environment (e.g., one in which barn façades are common, although what you are looking at is indeed a genuine barn).

With this distinction between two kinds of knowledge-undermining epistemic luck in mind, consider a variant on the case just described where the kind of epistemic luck that is at issue is specifically the environmental epistemic luck found in the Barney case. Here is the scenario:

Ethan
Ethan comes home to find his house in flames. He approaches someone who looks as if she is the fire officer in charge and asks her what the reason for the fire is. He is told by this person that the reason why his house is burning down is faulty wiring, and this coheres with his wider set of beliefs (e.g., about how faulty wiring can cause a house fire). The person Ethan is speaking to is indeed the fire officer in charge of this blaze, and what she says about the cause of the fire is both true and appropriately epistemically grounded (i.e., the fire officer *knows* that this is the cause of the fire). Crucially, however, all the other people in the vicinity who are dressed as fire officers are in fact on their way to a fancy dress party and have nothing to do with the fire brigade. Had Ethan asked one of them what the cause of the fire was, however, then they would have kept this fact from him and he would have believed their testimony.

In such a case, as we saw in chapter 3, the agent's cognitive success would be because of the agent's cognitive abilities, and yet the environmental epistemic luck at issue would prevent it from counting as knowledge. The critical question for us, however, is whether this is a case of understanding. I want to argue that it is, and thus that environmental epistemic luck, unlike standard Gettier-style intervening epistemic luck, *is* compatible with understanding. After all, Ethan has all the true beliefs required for understanding why his house burned down, and has also acquired this understanding in the right fashion. It is thus hard to see why the mere presence of environmental epistemic luck should deprive him of understanding.

So those commentators who argue that understanding is compatible with epistemic luck are only half-right. That is, they are right to think that understanding is compatible with a certain type of knowledge-undermining epistemic luck (i.e., of the sort found in the Ethan case), but wrong to think that it is compatible with *all* types of knowledge-undermining epistemic luck (such as the type of knowledge-undermining epistemic luck found in the Alexander case). Their mistake is thus to fail to distinguish between two crucial ways in which epistemic luck can be knowledge-undermining. That understanding is compatible with one type of knowledge-undermining epistemic luck suffices, however, to show that knowledge (even on an internalist construal) is distinct from understanding, since it entails that one can have understanding without the associated knowledge.

Interestingly, knowledge and understanding can also come apart in the opposite direction – i.e., there are also cases in which agents have knowledge while lacking the corresponding understanding. We can illustrate this point via an example of testimonial knowledge cast along the general lines of the Jenny case that we considered in chapter 3. Consider the following scenario:

> *Mandi*
> Mandi's house recently burned down because of faulty wiring. Mandi understands why her house burned down, knows why it burned down, and also knows that it burned down because of faulty wiring. Suppose now that her young son asks her why the house burned down and she tells him. On this basis, he forms the belief that his house burned down because of faulty wiring, even though he has no conception at all of how faulty wiring might cause a fire.

Does Mandi's son know why his house burned down? Intuitively, it would seem that he does. After all, Mandi has knowledge in this respect, and she is an excellent informant on matters like this. Indeed, we can imagine a teacher asking Mandi's son if he knows why his house burned down and him telling the teacher the reason. If asked by another teacher if Mandi's son knows why his house burned down, we could then imagine the first teacher saying that he did. Crucially, however, since Mandi's son lacks any conception of how faulty wiring might cause a house fire, we can hardly credit him with the corresponding understanding. Accordingly, it follows that not only can one have understanding without the corresponding knowledge, but also one can have knowledge without the corresponding understanding.

Understanding and cognitive achievement

In order to see why these conclusions about understanding are significant, it is worthwhile first reconsidering our discussion of the Barney and Jenny cases from chapter 3, and the challenge that they pose for robust virtue epistemology. Take the Barney case first. Note that this example in effect demonstrates that an agent can exhibit a cognitive achievement – at least in the weak sense described in chapter 7 that just involves cognitive success that is because of cognitive ability – even while failing to have the corresponding knowledge. After all, his cognitive success is primarily creditable to his cognitive ability; it is just that the environmental luck in play undermines his knowledge. Conversely, the Jenny case in effect demonstrates that an agent can gain knowledge even while failing to exhibit the corresponding cognitive achievement (in either the weak or the strong sense, where the latter, recall, in addition demands that one displays either a significantly high level of cognitive ability or that one overcomes a significant obstacle to cognitive success). After all, her cognitive success is not primarily creditable to her cognitive abilities at all, but to her knowledgeable informant. Knowledge thus comes apart from cognitive achievement (in both the strong and the weak sense).

Interestingly, however, the same is not true of understanding. Consider the three cases just given (Alexander, Ethan and Mandi). In the Alexander case the epistemic luck in play ensures that the agent does not exhibit a cognitive achievement, but then neither does he have the relevant understanding (or the relevant knowledge for that matter). In the Ethan case, in contrast (which recall is an analogue of the Barney case) the agent exhibits a cognitive achievement and possesses the relevant understanding, even while failing to possess the corresponding knowledge because of the environmental epistemic luck in play. Finally, in the Mandi case, which is an analogue of the Jenny case, the agent concerned – Mandi's son – gains knowledge while failing to exhibit the relevant cognitive achievement or possessing the corresponding understanding. In all cases, then, understanding is matching up with cognitive achievement in a way that knowledge isn't. This is, I suggest, no coincidence.

Indeed, the thesis that understanding is a type of cognitive achievement is independently very plausible. Its plausibility relates in part to the fact that understanding seems to be essentially an epistemically internalist notion, in the sense that if one has understanding, then it should not be opaque to one that that one has this understanding. In particular, one should have good reflectively accessible grounds in support of the relevant beliefs that undergird that understanding. But given that this is a requirement of understanding, it is unsurprising that one can construct a Jenny-style testimonial case in which an agent has knowledge but not understanding, since such cases work precisely by using examples of agents who, while having knowledge, lack good reflectively accessible grounds in favour of their beliefs. Relatedly, given that understanding involves a kind of cognitive responsibility in this way, it is not surprising that it is compatible with a variety of epistemic luck, since internalist notions more generally tend to be more compatible with epistemic luck than knowledge.

That understanding is both factive and resistant to standard Gettier-style epistemic luck also demonstrates, however, that we should be wary of construing understanding along purely internalist lines. One's reflectively accessible grounds in favour of one's belief might well survive the falsity of what one believes and also be compatible with Gettier-style luck, but as we have seen, the same is not true of understanding. Just as genuine cognitive achievements do not depend exclusively on the cognitive efforts of the agent, but also on the relevant cognitive success and the right connection obtaining between one's exercise of cognitive ability and cognitive success, so genuine understanding makes the same 'external' demands.

Understanding and final value

In the last chapter we noted a distinction between strong and weak achievements, which we saw was important to evaluating the case for the final value of knowledge offered by robust virtue epistemology (in answer to the tertiary value problem). Here is the distinction again:

Weak Achievement
A weak achievement is when a subject's success is because of (i.e., primarily creditable to) their exercise of relevant ability.

Strong Achievement
A strong achievement is when a subject's success is because of (i.e., primarily creditable to) their exercise of relevant ability, and where either (i) the subject is overcoming a significant obstacle to success, or (ii) the subject is displaying a significantly high level of relevant ability.

Recall that the point behind the distinction is that if one simply understands achievements as successes that are primarily creditable to one's abilities, then many achievements are very easy to come by, such as raising one's arm in normal conditions. And yet we don't tend to ordinarily use the notion of achievement in this permissive way, but rather reserve it for cases where either a significant obstacle is involved (e.g., where one's arm is in a cast), or where the success is achieved with ease but only because a hefty dose of ability is on display (e.g., when a skilled tennis player hits a tricky shot with ease). This distinction was important to our concerns in the last chapter because while it is *prima facie* plausible that knowledge might involve cognitive achievements in the weak sense, it was not nearly so plausible that it might involve achievements in the strong sense. And yet it is only achievements in the strong sense that are credible candidates for final value, so it is only if knowledge involves strong achievements that one has a route from robust virtue epistemology to the final value of knowledge.

The manner in which this debate relates to our current concerns is that a convincing case can be made that understanding essentially involves achievements in the strong sense. If that's right, then although robust virtue epistemology failed to offer a plausible account of the final value of knowledge, we might nonetheless have a route to showing that there is an epistemic standing, in the general ballpark of knowledge, which is distinctively valuable in the manner that we supposed knowledge to be – i.e., understanding. Typically, after all, one gains understanding by undertaking an obstacle-overcoming effort to piece together the relevant pieces of information. Moreover, where understanding is gained with ease, this will be because of the fact that one is bringing to bear significant cognitive ability. Perhaps, for example, in coming across one's house in flames one is immediately able to gain an understanding of why this event is occurring because one is able to observe some crucial feature of the event taking place before one which, along, say, with the relevant background information that one possesses, definitively indicates how this event came about in such a way as to afford one the relevant understanding. But here the spontaneity of the understanding is entirely due to the exercise of significant cognitive ability, and hence poses no challenge to the idea that understanding specifically involves cognitive achievement along the lines set out by the strong account of the achievement thesis.

This last point is significant, since it lends support to the claim that understanding is distinctively valuable. As we noted above, the strong account of the achievement thesis is very plausible, as is the claim that achievements, so understood, are in their nature finally valuable (where this means that they are *prima facie* valuable). Once we couple these claims to the thesis that understanding involves cognitive achievement in the relevant sense, understanding will inherit the final value of this kind of achievement. Moreover, given that it is specific to cognitive achievements, so construed, to be finally valuable in this way, it follows that there won't be a lesser epistemic standing that is just as valuable.

Understanding, then, is more valuable than lesser epistemic standings not just as a matter of degree but of kind.

Concluding remarks

So while we have argued that knowledge lacks final value and so is not distinctively valuable in the way that we intuitively suppose, we have also claimed that understanding, at least when conceived of properly at any rate, *is* distinctively (and hence finally) valuable. If this is right, then this should give us pause to wonder whether we are right to place knowledge at the centre of epistemological theorising in the way that we do. Perhaps, that is, we should focus instead on 'higher' epistemic standings like understanding instead. This would not mean that an exploration of knowledge would no longer be important, just that this project would become less central to epistemological inquiry.

Note that this would also have ramifications for a number of debates within epistemology. To take one example, consider the problem of radical scepticism that we looked at in chapter 6. If understanding, unlike knowledge, is a distinctively valuable epistemic standing, then shouldn't we be considering the sceptical problem as it applies to this epistemic standing rather than knowledge? In particular, notice that merely responding to the sceptical problem as applied to knowledge would not provide one with any great comfort if a sister sceptical problem as applied to understanding remained unresolved.

So while this textbook reflects the current state of epistemology, which has the analysis of knowledge at its heart, it should also be thought of as encouraging the reader to usher in a new era of epistemology that reflects broader epistemic concerns.

Chapter summary

We began by noting the very different usages of the notion of understanding. In particular, this notion can be applied to whole subject matters or to specific issues. Our focus in this chapter has been on the latter, on the assumption that in gaining a grip on this notion of understanding we thereby gain a grip on the notion more generally. In particular, we have focussed on *causal understanding*, which is understanding of the cause of a specific event. On the standard view about causal understanding in the philosophy of science, to understand why an event happened is to know why that event happened, which is in turn to have propositional knowledge of the cause of that event. We also noted that understanding, at least in the causal sense, is generally regarded to be *factive*, and that it plausibly also entails an epistemic internalist aspect. We then considered some cases. The 'Alexander' case purported to show that intervening epistemic luck undermines causal understanding just as it undermines (propositional) knowledge. In contrast, the 'Ethan' case purported to show that, in contrast to (propositional) knowledge, environmental epistemic luck is compatible with knowledge. The 'Mandi' case was meant to show that there are cases in which a subject can have causal knowledge without the corresponding causal understanding. These claims are important because they potentially show that causal knowledge and causal understanding come apart from one another in both directions (and hence that causal understanding is not a species of knowledge). This point has ramifications for the debate about epistemic value, in that while it is implausible that weak cognitive achievements are finally valuable, it is plausible that strong cognitive achievements are valuable. And yet it is credible that causal understanding – and perhaps understanding in general – essentially involves strong cognitive achievements. Thus, it could be that the right way to respond to the problem of the value of knowledge is not by defending the final value of knowledge but rather by advocating the final value of a distinct epistemic standing: understanding.

Further introductory reading

For a helpful overview of recent work on understanding, see Grimm (2011). For an overview of the specific topic of the value of understanding, see Grimm (2012). For an annotated bibliography on recent on this topic, see Grimm & Hannon (2014). See also Pritchard & Turri (2014), which is listed below under free internet resources. For an accessible account of the nature and value of achievements, see Pritchard (2010a).

Further advanced reading

For a useful critical discussion of the standard view of causal understanding in philosophy of science, see Grimm (2006). For some key discussions of understanding, see Zagzebski (2001), Kvanvig (2003; 2009), and Pritchard (2009). See also the exchange between Grimm (2014) and Pritchard (2014). For an in-depth discussion of the some of the issues raised in this chapter, see Haddock, Millar & Pritchard (2010, chs. 1–4). For an exploration of how the debate regarding the value of knowledge can have an impact on our understanding of the problem of radical scepticism, see Pritchard (2008c).

Free internet resources

See Pritchard & Turri (2014) for a detailed account of the nature and value of understanding in the context of the general topic of epistemic value. See the 'Study of Understanding' webpage (http://www.studyofunderstanding.com) – maintained by Stephen Grimm – for lots of interesting materials on the nature of understanding, from a range of disciplinary perspectives.

Study questions

1. Describe in your own words the distinction between holistic and non-holistic uses of the notion of understanding. Give at least two examples of your own of each.
2. Why is it more plausible that the holistic usage of the notion of understanding (as opposed to the non-holistic usage) is non-factive? What do you think of the idea that the non-holistic usage of the notion of understanding is factive?
3. What do you think of the proposal that understanding is an essentially internalist notion?
4. Describe, in your own words, what causal understanding is. Try to give a couple of examples of your own of this kind of understanding.
5. Is causal understanding compatible with intervening epistemic luck?
6. Is causal understanding compatible with environmental epistemic luck?
7. Can one know why such-and-such happened even while lacking the corresponding causal understanding?
8. What is the relationship between knowledge and understanding? Is understanding a kind of knowledge? Or is understanding distinct from knowing (i.e., in the sense that these two notions can come apart in both directions)?
9. Does understanding essentially involve cognitive achievements? If so, does it essentially involve strong cognitive achievements, or only weak cognitive achievements?
10. Does understanding have a special kind of value (i.e., final value)? In particular, does it have a special kind of value that knowledge lacks?
11. What do you think of the suggestion that understanding ought to be the proper focus of epistemological theorizing, rather than knowledge? Do you find this persuasive? Do you think some other epistemic standing should be the proper focus of epistemological theorizing (or that there should be a multitude of foci)?

Sample essay questions

1. Critically evaluate the claim that understanding is a kind of knowledge. Is such a claim defensible, do you think?
2. 'Understanding is finally valuable.' Discuss.
3. Does understanding essentially involve cognitive achievement? If it does, what implications, if any, might this have for epistemology?

Bibliography

Axtell, G. (1997). 'Recent Work in Virtue Epistemology', *American Philosophical Quarterly* 34, 1–27.
—— (2007). 'Two For the Show: Anti-Luck and Virtue Epistemologies in Consonance', *Synthese* 158, 363–83.
Baehr, J. (2004). 'Virtue Epistemology', *Internet Encyclopædia Philosophy*, (eds) B. Dowden & J. Fieser, http://www.iep.utm.edu/v/VirtueEp.htm.
Battaly, H. (2008). 'Virtue Epistemology', *Philosophy Compass* 3, 639–63.
Becker, K. (2013). 'Modal Epistemology', *Oxford Bibliographies: Philosophy*, (ed.) D. H. Pritchard, DOI: 10.1093/OBO/9780195396577–0139.
Black, T. (2002). 'A Moorean Response to Brain-In-A-Vat Scepticism', *Australasian Journal of Philosophy* 80, 148–63.
—— (2003). 'Contextualism in Epistemology', *Internet Encyclopædia of Philosophy*, (eds) B. Dowden & J. Fieser, www.iep.utm.edu/c/contextu.htm.
—— (2011). 'Modal and Anti-Luck Epistemology', *Routledge Companion to Epistemology*, (eds) S. Bernecker & D. H. Pritchard, 187–98, Routledge, London.
Chisholm, R. M. (1989). *The Theory of Knowledge*, (3rd edn), Prentice Hall, Englewood Cliffs, NJ.
Cohen, S. (1998). 'Contextualist Solutions to Epistemological Problems: Scepticism, Gettier and the Lottery', *Australasian Journal of Philosophy* 76, 289–306.
—— (2000). 'Contextualism and Skepticism', *Philosophical Issues* 10, 94–107.
Conee, E., & Feldman, R. (2004). *Evidentialism*, Oxford University Press, Oxford.
Craig, E. (1991). *Knowledge and the State of Nature*, Oxford University Press, Oxford.
DeRose, K. (1995). 'Solving the Skeptical Problem', *Philosophical Review* 104, 1–52.
Dretske, F. (1970). 'Epistemic Operators', *Journal of Philosophy* 67, 1007–23.
—— (2014a). 'The Case Against Closure', *Contemporary Debates in Epistemology* (2nd edn), (eds) E. Sosa, M. Steup & J. Turri, 27–40, Blackwell, Oxford.
—— (2014b). 'Reply to Hawthorne', *Contemporary Debates in Epistemology* (2nd edn), (eds) E. Sosa, M. Steup & J. Turri, 56–59, Blackwell, Oxford.
Engel, M. (2011). 'Epistemic Luck', *Internet Encyclopaedia of Philosophy*, (eds) J. Fieser & B. Dowden, http://www.iep.utm.edu/epi–luck/.
Gettier, E. (1963). 'Is Justified True Belief Knowledge?', *Analysis* 23, 121–3.
Gibbons, J. (2006). 'Access Externalism', *Mind* 115, 19–39.
Goldberg, S. (2010). 'Semantic Externalism', *Oxford Bibliographies: Philosophy*, (ed.) D. H. Pritchard, DOI: 10.1093/OBO/9780195396577–0113.
Goldman, A. (1976). 'Discrimination and Perceptual Knowledge', *Journal of Philosophy* 73, 771–91.
—— (1986). *Epistemology and Cognition*, Harvard University Press, Cambridge, MA.
—— (2007). 'Philosophical Intuitions: Their Target, Their Source, and Their Epistemic Status', *Philosophical Knowledge: Its Possibility and Scope*, (eds) C. Beyer & A. Burri, 1–26, Rodopi, Amsterdam.

Graham, P. (2011). 'Epistemic Justification', *Oxford Bibliographies: Philosophy*, (ed.) D. H. Pritchard, DOI: 10.1093/OBO/9780195396577-0060.

Greco, J. (1999). 'Agent Reliabilism', *Philosophical Perspectives* 13, 273–96.

—— (2000). *Putting Skeptics in Their Place: The Nature of Skeptical Arguments and Their Role in Philosophical Inquiry*, Cambridge University Press, Cambridge.

—— (2007). 'Worries About Pritchard's Safety', *Synthese* 158, 299–302.

—— (2008). 'What's Wrong With Contextualism?', *Philosophical Quarterly* 58, 416–36.

—— (2009a). *Achieving Knowledge: A Virtue-Theoretic Account of Epistemic Normativity*, Cambridge: Cambridge University Press.

—— (2009b). 'The Value Problem', *Epistemic Value*, (eds) A. Haddock, A. Millar & D. H. Pritchard, 313–21, Oxford University Press, Oxford.

—— (2011). 'The Value Problem', *Routledge Companion to Epistemology*, (eds) S. Bernecker & D. H. Pritchard, 219–32, Routledge, London.

Greco, J., & Turri, J. (2011). 'Virtue Epistemology', *Stanford Encyclopædia of Philosophy*, (ed.) E. Zalta, http://plato.stanford.edu/entries/epistemology-virtue/.

Grice, P. (1989). *Studies in the Way of Words*, Harvard University Press, Cambridge MA.

Grimm, S. (2006). 'Is Understanding a Species of Knowledge?', *British Journal for the Philosophy of Science* 57, 515–36.

—— (2011). 'Understanding', *Routledge Companion to Epistemology*, (eds) S. Bernecker & D. H. Pritchard, 84–94, Routledge, London.

—— (2012). 'The Value of Understanding', *Philosophy Compass* 7, 103–17.

—— (2014). 'Understanding as Knowledge of Causes', *Virtue Scientia: Bridges Between Virtue Epistemology and Philosophy of Science*, (ed.) A. Fairweather, 329–46, Springer, Dordrecht, Holland.

Grimm, S., & Hannon, M. (2014). 'Understanding', *Oxford Bibliographies: Philosophy*, (ed.) D. H. Pritchard, DOI: 10.1093/OBO/9780195396577-0121.

Hawthorne, J. (2004). *Knowledge and Lotteries*, Oxford University Press, Oxford.

—— (2014). 'The Case for Closure', *Contemporary Debates in Epistemology* (2nd edn), (eds) E. Sosa, M. Steup & J. Turri, 40–43–56, Blackwell, Oxford.

Hetherington, S. (2005). 'Gettier Problems', *Internet Encyclopaedia of Philosophy*, (eds) B. Dowden & J. Fieser, http://www.iep.utm.edu/g/gettier.htm.

—— (2011). 'The Gettier Problem', *Routledge Companion to Epistemology*, (eds) S. Bernecker & D. H. Pritchard, 119–30, Routledge, London.

—— (2014). 'There Can be Lucky Knowledge', *Contemporary Debates in Epistemology* (2nd edn), (eds) E. Sosa, M. Steup & J. Turri, 164–76, Blackwell, Oxford.

—— (2015). 'Knowledge', *Internet Encyclopaedia of Philosophy*, (eds) B. Dowden & J. Fieser, http://www.iep.utm.edu/knowledg/.

Ichikawa, J. J., & Steup, M. (2012). 'The Analysis of Knowledge', *Stanford Encyclopædia of Philosophy*, (ed.) E. Zalta, http://plato.stanford.edu/entries/knowledge-analysis/.

Kallestrup, J. (2011). *Semantic Externalism*, Routledge, London.

Kallestrup, J., & Pritchard, D. H. (2013). 'Robust Virtue Epistemology and Epistemic Dependence', *Knowledge, Virtue and Action: Putting Epistemic Virtues to Work*, (eds) T. Henning & D. Schweikard, ch. 11, Routledge, London.

—— (2014). 'Virtue Epistemology and Epistemic Twin Earth', *European Journal of Philosophy* 22, 335–57.

Klein, P. (2015). 'Skepticism', *Stanford Encyclopædia of Philosophy*, (ed.) E. Zalta, http://plato.stanford.edu/entries/skepticism/.

Kornblith, H. (ed.) (2001). *Epistemology: Internalism and Externalism*, Blackwell, Oxford.

—— (2007). 'Naturalism and Intuitions', *Philosophical Knowledge: Its Possibility and Scope*, (eds) C. Beyer & A. Burri, 27–50, Rodopi, Amsterdam.

Kusch, M. (2009). 'Testimony and the Value of Knowledge', *Epistemic Value*, (eds) A. Haddock, A. Millar & D. H. Pritchard, 60–94, Oxford University Press, Oxford.

Kvanvig, J. (1992). *The Intellectual Virtues and the Life of the Mind: On the Place of the Virtues in Contemporary Epistemology*, Rowman & Littlefield, Savage, MD.

—— (2003). The *Value of Knowledge and the Pursuit of Understanding*, Cambridge University Press, Cambridge.

—— (2009). 'The Value of Understanding', *Epistemic Value*, (eds) A. Haddock, A. Millar & D. H. Pritchard, 95–111, Oxford University Press, Oxford.

—— (2011). 'Virtue Epistemology', *Routledge Companion to Epistemology*, (eds) S. Bernecker & D. H. Pritchard, 199–207, Routledge, London.

Lackey, J. (2007). 'Why We Don't Deserve Credit for Everything We Know', *Synthese* 158, 345–61.

—— (2008). 'What Luck Is Not', *Australasian Journal of Philosophy* 86, 255–67.

Lau, J., & Deutsch, M. (2014). 'Externalism about Mental Content', *Stanford Encyclopaedia of Philosophy*, (ed.) E. Zalta, http://plato.stanford.edu/entries/content-externalism/.

Lehrer, K. (1965). 'Knowledge, Truth and Evidence', *Analysis* 25, 168–75.

Lehrer, K., & Cohen, S. (1983). 'Justification, Truth, and Coherence', *Synthese* 55, 191–207.

Lewis, D. (1996). 'Elusive Knowledge', *Australasian Journal of Philosophy* 74, 549–67.

Loux, M. (ed.). (1979). *The Possible and the Actual*, Cornell University Press, Ithaca, NJ.

McDowell, J. (1995). 'Knowledge and the Internal', *Philosophy and Phenomenological Research*, 55, 877–93.

McGlynn, A. (2014). *Knowledge First?* Palgrave Macmillan, London.

Millar, A. (2008). 'Perceptual-Recognitional Abilities and Perceptual Knowledge', *Disjunctivism: Perception, Action, Knowledge*, (eds) A. Haddock & F. Macpherson, 330–47, Oxford University Press, Oxford.

Moore, G. E. (1925). 'A Defence of Common Sense', *Contemporary British Philosophy* (2nd series), (ed.) J. H. Muirhead, Allen & Unwin, London.

—— (1939). 'Proof of an External World', *Proceedings of the British Academy* 25, 273–300.

—— (1959). 'Certainty', in his *Philosophical Papers*, Allen & Unwin, London.

Neta, R. (2008). 'In Defense of Disjunctivism, *Disjunctivism: Perception, Action, Knowledge*, (eds) A. Haddock & F. Macpherson, 311–29, Oxford University Press, Oxford.

Neta, R. & Pritchard, D. H. (2007). 'McDowell and the New Evil Genius', *Philosophy and Phenomenological Research* 74, 381–96.

Nozick, R. (1981). *Philosophical Explanations*, Oxford University Press, Oxford.

Olsson, E. (2013). 'The Value of Knowledge', *Oxford Bibliographies: Philosophy*, (ed.) D. H. Pritchard, DOI: 10.1093/OBO/9780195396577-0008.

Pappas, G. (2014). 'Internalist vs. Externalist Conceptions of Epistemic Justification', *Stanford Encyclopaedia of Philosophy*, (ed.) E. Zalta http://plato.stanford.edu/entries/justep-intext/.

Plantinga, A. (1993). *Warrant and Proper Function*, Oxford University Press, Oxford.

Poston, T. (2008). 'Internalism and Externalism in Epistemology', *Internet Encyclopaedia of Philosophy*, (eds) J. Fieser & B. Dowden, http://www.iep.utm.edu/int-ext/.

Pritchard, D. H. (2002a). 'Recent Work on Radical Skepticism', *American Philosophical Quarterly* 39, 215–57.

—— (2002b). 'Resurrecting the Moorean Response to the Sceptic', *International Journal of Philosophical Studies* 10, 283–307.

—— (2002c). 'Skepticism, Contemporary', *Internet Encyclopaedia of Philosophy*, (eds) B. Dowden & J. Fieser, http://www.iep.utm.edu/s/skepcont.htm.

—— (2005). *Epistemic Luck*, Oxford University Press, Oxford.

—— (2007a). 'Anti-Luck Epistemology', *Synthese* 158, 277–98.

—— (2007b). 'How to be a Neo-Moorean', *Internalism and Externalism in Semantics and Epistemology*, (ed.) S. Goldberg, Oxford University Press, Oxford.

—— (2007c). 'Recent Work on Epistemic Value', *American Philosophical Quarterly* 44, 85–110.

—— (2008a). 'McDowellian Neo-Mooreanism', *Disjunctivism: Perception, Action, Knowledge*, (eds) A. Haddock & F. Macpherson, 283–310, Oxford University Press, Oxford.

—— (2008b). 'Radical Scepticism, Epistemic Luck and Epistemic Value', *Proceedings and Addresses of the Aristotelian Society (suppl. vol.)* 82, 19–41.

—— (2008c). 'Safety, Sensitivity and Anti-Luck Epistemology', *Oxford Handbook of Skepticism*, (ed.) J. Greco, 437–55, Oxford University Press, Oxford.

—— (2009a). 'Knowledge', *Central Issues in Philosophy*, (ed.) J. Shand, 24–36, Blackwell, Oxford.

—— (2009b). 'Knowledge, Understanding and Epistemic Value', *Epistemology (Royal Institute of Philosophy Lectures)*, (ed.) A. O'Hear, 19–43, Cambridge University Press, Cambridge.

—— (2009c). 'Wright *Contra* McDowell on Perceptual Knowledge and Scepticism', *Synthese* 171, 467–79.

—— (2010a). 'Achievements, Luck and Value', *Think* 25, 1–12.

—— (2010b). 'Contemporary Skepticism', *Oxford Bibliographies: Philosophy*, (ed.) D. H. Pritchard, DOI: 10.1093/OBO/9780195396577-0109.

—— (2011). 'Evidentialism, Internalism, Disjunctivism', *Evidentialism and its Discontents*, (ed.) T. Dougherty, 362–92, Oxford University Press, Oxford.

—— (2012a). 'Anti-Luck Virtue Epistemology', *Journal of Philosophy* 109, 247–79.

—— (2012b). *Epistemological Disjunctivism*, Oxford University Press, Oxford.

—— (2012c). 'On Meta-Epistemology', *Harvard Review of Philosophy* 18, 91–108.

—— (2013). *What is this Thing Called Knowledge?* (3rd edn), Routledge, London.

—— (2014a). 'Knowledge and Understanding', *Virtue Scientia: Bridges Between Virtue Epistemology and Philosophy of Science*, (ed.) A. Fairweather, 315–28, Springer, Dordrecht, Holland.

—— (2014b). 'The Modal Account of Luck', *Metaphilosophy* 45, 594–619.

—— (2014c). 'There Cannot be Lucky Knowledge', *Contemporary Debates in Epistemology* (2nd edn), (eds) M. Steup, J. Turri & E. Sosa, 152–64, Blackwell, Oxford.

—— (2015a). 'Anti-Luck Epistemology and the Gettier Problem', *Philosophical Studies* 172, 93–111.
—— (2015b). *Epistemic Angst: Radical Skepticism and the Groundlessness of Our Believing*, Princeton University Press, Princeton, NJ.
—— (Ed.) (2015c). *What is this Thing Called Philosophy?* Routledge, London.
—— (Forthcoming a). 'Epistemic *Angst*', *Philosophy and Phenomenological Research*.
—— (Forthcoming b). 'Knowledge, Luck and Virtue: Resolving the Gettier Problem', *The Gettier Problem*, (eds) C. Almeida, P. Klein & R. Borges, Oxford University Press, Oxford.
Pritchard, D. H., Millar, A., & Haddock, A. (2010). *The Nature and Value of Knowledge: Three Investigations*, Oxford University Press, Oxford.
Pritchard, D. H., & Smith, M. (2004). 'The Psychology and Philosophy of Luck', *New Ideas in Psychology* 22, 1–28.
Pritchard, D. H., & Turri, J. (2014). 'The Value of Knowledge', *Stanford Encyclopaedia of Philosophy*, (ed.) E. Zalta, http://plato.stanford.edu/entries/knowledge-value/.
Pritchard, D. H., & Whittington, L. (2015). *The Philosophy of Luck*, Blackwell, Oxford.
Riggs, W. (2007). 'Why Epistemologists are so Down on Their Luck', *Synthese* 158, 329–44.
Rysiew, P. (2007). 'Epistemic Contextualism', *Stanford Encyclopaedia of Philosophy*, (ed.) E. Zalta, http://plato.stanford.edu/entries/contextualism-epistemology/.
—— (2011). 'Contextualism', *Routledge Companion to Epistemology*, (eds) S. Bernecker & D. H. Pritchard, 523–35, Routledge, London.
Smith, B. (2013). 'Internalism and Externalism in the Philosophy of Mind and Language', *Internet Encyclopaedia of Philosophy*, (eds) J. Fieser & B. Dowden, http://www.iep.utm.edu/int-ex-ml/.
Sosa, E. (1991). *Knowledge in Perspective: Selected Essays in Epistemology*, Cambridge University Press, Cambridge.
—— (1999). 'How to Defeat Opposition to Moore', *Philosophical Perspectives* 13, 141–54.
—— (2000). 'Skepticism and Contextualism', *Philosophical Issues* 10, 1–18.
—— (2007). *A Virtue Epistemology: Apt Belief and Reflective Knowledge*, Oxford University Press, Oxford.
—— (2009). *Reflective Knowledge: Apt Belief and Reflective Knowledge*, Oxford University Press, Oxford.
—— (2011). *Knowing Full Well*, Princeton, NJ: Princeton University Press.
—— (2015). *Judgment and Agency*, Oxford University Press, Oxford.
Stanley, J. (2005). *Knowledge and Practical Interests*, Clarendon Press, Oxford.
Steup, M. (2005). 'Epistemology', *Stanford Encyclopædia of Philosophy*, (ed.) E. Zalta, http://plato.stanford.edu/entries/epistemology/.
Stine, G. C. (1976). 'Skepticism, Relevant Alternatives, and Deductive Closure', *Philosophical Studies* 29, 249–61.
Truncellito, D. (2007). 'Epistemology', *Internet Encyclopaedia of Philosophy*, (eds) B. Dowden & J. Fieser, http://www.iep.utm.edu/e/epistemo.htm.
Turri, J. (2011). 'Knowledge', *Oxford Bibliographies: Philosophy*, (ed.) D. H. Pritchard, DOI: 10.1093/OBO/9780195396577–0062.

Turri, J., & Sosa, E. (2010). 'Virtue Epistemology', *Oxford Bibliographies: Philosophy*, (ed.) D. H. Pritchard, DOI: 10.1093/OBO/9780195396577-0123.

Unger, P. (1968). 'An Analysis of Factual Knowledge', *Journal of Philosophy* 65, 157–70.

—— (1975). *Ignorance: A Case for Scepticism*, Clarendon Press, Oxford.

Weatherson, B. (2003). 'What Good Are Counterexamples?', *Philosophical Studies* 115, 1–31.

Williams, B. (2004). *Truth and Truthfulness: An Essay in Genealogy*, Princeton University Press, Princeton, NJ.

Williams, M. (1991). *Unnatural Doubts: Epistemological Realism and the Basis of Scepticism*, Blackwell, Oxford.

Williamson, T. (2000). *Knowledge and its Limits*, Oxford University Press, Oxford.

Zagzebski, L. (1996). *Virtues of the Mind: An Inquiry into the Nature of Virtue and the Ethical Foundations of Knowledge*, Cambridge University Press, Cambridge.

—— (1999). 'What is Knowledge?', *The Blackwell Guide to Epistemology*, (eds) J. Greco & E. Sosa, 92–116, Blackwell, Oxford.

—— (2001). 'Recovering Understanding', *Knowledge, Truth, and Obligation: Essays on Epistemic Justification, Virtue, and Responsibility*, (ed.) M. Steup, Oxford University Press, Oxford.

Index

ability intuition, 4–6, 14, 15, 17, 19, 34, 37–41, 44, 49, 59, 63–64, 72, 74–76
accessibilism, 78–90
achievement, 52–54, 60, 62, 65, 108–125, 126, 131–38
anti-luck epistemology, 18–42, 48, 50, 63–65, 67, 69–70, 75–76
anti-luck intuition, 5, 7, 14–15, 17–19, 23, 30, 34, 36, 39–41, 43–44, 49, 59, 63–64, 71, 75
anti-luck virtue epistemology, 63–76, 87–88, 108
Axtell, G. 61

Baehr, J., 61
Battaly, H., 60
Becker, K., 41, 75
Black, T., 41, 110

Chisholm, R. M., 16
classical account of knowledge, 3–17, 19, 49
closure-based sceptical argument, 92–111
closure principle, 95–103, 109–111
Cohen, S., 41, 90, 110
Conee, E., 90
content externalism/internalism, 81–91
contextualism, 100–111
Craig, E., 16, 75

DeRose, K., 110
Deutsch, M., 90
Dretske, F., 41, 110

Engel, M., 41
environmental epistemic luck, 53–62, 64, 70, 129–32, 136–37
epistemic externalism/internalism, 10–17, 19, 40–41, 48, 61, 77–91, 110
epistemic value, 112–25, 126, 133–37

epistemological disjunctivism, 83–90, 108

Feldman, R., 90

Gettier, E., 3, 6, 16, 116
Gettier problem *see* Gettier-style cases
Gettier-style cases, 3–18, 23, 28, 40–43, 49–54, 60, 62, 65, 67, 119–20, 129–33
Gibbons, J., 90
Goldberg, S., 89
Goldman, A., 16, 61
Graham, P., 89
Greco, J.. 41, 61, 76, 124
Grimm, S., 136, 137

Haddock, A., 61, 75, 124, 136
Hannon, M., 136
Hawthorne, J., 110
Hetherington, S., 16, 41

Ichikawa, J. J., 16, 41
infallibilism, 95, 110

Justification, 5–17, 19, 34, 46–48, 68, 77–80, 84, 88–91, 115–16, 128–29

Kallestrup, J., 61, 75, 90
Klein, P., 110, 111
Kornblith, H., 16, 90
Kusch, M., 76
Kvanvig, J., 60, 61, 124, 136

Lackey, J., 61
Lau, J., 90
Lehrer, K., 16, 90
Lewis, D., 41, 110
lottery problem, 23–24, 28–33, 40–42
Loux, M., 41

McDowell, J., 90
mentalism, 78–90

Millar, A., 61, 75, 124, 136
Moore, G. E., 104, 110

neo-Mooreanism, 104–111
new evil genius intuition, 80–86, 90–91
no false lemmas, 9–17
Nozick, R., 41, 110

Olsson, E., 124

Pappas, G., 90
Plantinga, A., 61
Plato, 113, 123, 124
possible worlds, 20–24, 25–42, 54–57, 97–99, 105–06
Poston, T., 89, 90
Pritchard, D. H., 16, 41, 60, 61, 75, 90, 110, 111, 124, 136, 137

relevant alternatives, 94–95
reliabilism, 13–16, 43–50, 59–62, 68–69, 89
Rysiew, P., 110

safety principle, 24, 26–42, 63–69, 75–76, 96, 98, 106
sceptical hypotheses, 93–111
scepticism, 26, 92–111, 124, 135–36
sensitivity principle, 19–33, 40–42, 64, 96–99, 105, 109–11

Smith, B., 90
Socrates, 113, 114, 116, 123, 124
Sosa, E., 41, 60, 61, 75, 110
Stanley, J., 110
Steup, M., 16, 41
Stine, G. C., 110
swamping problem, 113–16, 123–25

testimony, 25, 58, 73, 130
Truncellito, D., 16
Turri, J., 16, 60, 61, 75, 76, 124, 136, 137

understanding, 126–38
Unger, P., 41, 110

value, final/instrumental, 118–25, 125, 126, 133–38
virtue epistemology, 43–62, 63–76, 87–88, 108, 118–25, 131–34
virtue reliabilism, 44–50, 59–62, 68–69
virtue responsibilism, 46–51, 60–62, 65, 69

Weatherson, B., 16
Whittington, L., 41
Williams, B., 76
Williams, M., 110
Williamson, T., 16, 41, 90

Zagzebski, L., 16, 61, 136